TABLE OF CONTENTS

Introduction

This book is the continuation of the Judgement Day series. In the previous book, we have talked about the Trumpet, the Hashr, land of Hashr, the Shafa'a of Prophet SAW, including various categories of Shafa'a.

Now, we will continue from where we left off. We're going chronologically This book begins the next section of this series. Which is going to be a very, very detailed discussion of this topic, that will turn to the Quran and Sunnah. And we'll discuss what we know about one of the most fundamental pillars of our religion. That is the Day of Judgement itself.

Day of Judgement, in fact, is one of the fundamental pillars that this whole religion is based upon. The three pillars are belief in Allah SWT, belief in the Prophet AS and belief in Judgement Day. These are the three fundamentals of all fundamentals.

So, we begin our discussion about the reality of Qiyamah. And we'll discuss what we know about Qiyamah. And what Allah SWT has mentioned of it. In this book we will move up until the very end, which is when people will be taken to their final destination. Either Jannah, may Allah SWT make us amongst them. Or Jahannam, we seek Allah SWT's refuge from that.

Then when we finish this part of our discussion, then after that we will begin a discussion of the two Dar ul Akhira; either Jannah, may Allah SWT make us amongst them, or description of Jahannam, so that we can be aware of it. So, this will be the third book in series about the Qiyamah.

Coming of Allah SWT on Judgement Day

So, when discussing the day of judgement, we have learned about the concept of Shafa'a, and the Shafa'a of the Prophet SAW, and different types of Shafa'a. But what began all of that discussion was the Grand Shafa'a or Maqam Al Mahmood of our Prophet SAW. That was the Shafa'a to begin the day of judgment. The Shafa'a to begin the Hisab after everyone in resurrected and gathered in Ard al Mahshar.

Since we're discussing that first Shafa'a, we did all types of Shafa'a together chronologically to the Shafa'a. But not all Shafa'a are going to happen on the day of judgement. They are going to happen eons later. It's going to happen after a time frame we don't even know about.

Now, we go back to that hadith of our Prophet SAW, where he was bowing down in front of the Throne of Allah SWT and Allah SWT says, "O Muhammad SAW raise up your head. Speak, you should be listened to. Ask you shall be granted what you want. And then give the Shafa'a". This will be the beginning of the Judgment, on the day of judgement.

The next thing that will happen after Allah SWT accepts Prophet SAW's Shafa'a to begin the day of judgement, according the Quran and Sunnah, is that Allah SWT is himself going to come to the plains of the day of judgment. And the Quran is very explicit about this. It is something that the believers' heart should tremble at. When they hear about this aspect, the Iman should quiver.

Allah SWT will descend down, and he will come in a large gathering of Angels. The Quran mentioned in the number of verses that Allah SWT will come on the day of judgment to begin the Judgment itself. For example, Allah SWT says in the Quran, "Know on that day, remember the day that the Earth itself will be levelled and pounded and crushed; and your Lord shall come, and the Angels will come row after row". This Ayah is from Surah Al Fajr.

Allah SWT mentions in Surah Al-Baqarah verse 210, after he mentions the punishment for those who reject Allah SWT, and Allah SWT threatens them and tells them to repent and accept Islam; then Allah SWT asks a rhetorical question, "What are they waiting for? What is going to cause them to repent? Are they waiting for the time that Allah SWT himself is going to come? Allah SWT is going to come in the shadows of many clouds, surrounded with the Angels; And the matter shall be settled. And all affairs shall turn to Allah SWT and return to Allah SWT".

In Surah Al An'am verse number 158, once again in the context of threatening those who reject the religion and those who reject the day of judgement, Allah SWT is telling them, "What will cause you to repent? What are you waiting for? What will cause you to wake up and realize that there is something that's going to happen after this life? Life after death is going to happen. Are they waiting that the Angels, all of them come down? Or are they waiting for Allah SWT to himself to come? Or are they waiting for some of the signs of Allah SWT to come?"

In other words, it is very clear that Allah SWT is saying that there will come a time when all of the Angels will come, and there will come a time when Allah SWT himself will come. Also, on that point in time, Jahannam will be brought out.

In the famous Hadith in Tirmidhi, the Prophet SAW said, "On the day of judgment Allah SWT will come down to his servants to judge between all of them". This is an authentic Hadith where our Prophet SAW is explicitly saying that on the day of judgement Allah SWT himself is going to come and decide between all of his creation.

There is also a verse in the Quran that is used by some of the earliest scholars of Islam to affirm this concept of Allah SWT himself a coming down on the day of judgment and that is the verse in Surah As Zumar, "And on that day the Earth is going to be lightened up by the light of Allah SWT. The Noor of Allah SWT will make this whole earth lighten up. And the book of deeds is going to be brought down and placed. And the Prophets AS will be brought and all of the witnesses will be brought, and the matter shall be settled".

At Tabari RA, the famous Mufassir of the Quran, in his book of tafseer says that, "The Earth shall be lightened up by the light of its Lord. That is going to happen when Ar-Rehman himself comes in order to judge between his creation". He brings in a number of traditions from the early Companions and the early Sahaba.

For example, Al Hassan Al Basri RA said that, "When it is the day of judgement, Our Lord Shall appear, so that the entire creation will see him. But the Kafir will be veiled from him".

Imam Al Baghawi RA said, "The Earth shall lighten up by the light of its Lord. this is going to happen when Allah SWR himself will come and appear in front of his Creation in order to judge between all of them".

Believers Seeing Allah SWT

Now, when the Quran mention that Allah SWT is going to come down, it obviously means that the believers will see Allah SWT. This shall give us a sense of hope and expectation and fear all combined. That is exactly what the Quran mentions. This is again very explicit in the Quran and in the Sunnah.

In Surah Qiyamah Allah SWT says, "On that day, the day of judgment, the Believers', their faces will be happy and excited, shining bright. Because there are seeing Allah SWT". This is the greatest blessing for the believers, and this blessing it will happen on multiple occasions on the day of judgment. But this shall be the first time that the believers see Allah SWT.

The Quran and Sunnah are very clear that Allah SWT will bless the believers to see him. It is something that we ask Allah SWT for. Ameen! Allah SWT says in the Quran, "Those who do good deeds, they shall get Jannah and they shall get more than Jannah itself". Allah SWT says in Surah Kahf verse 35, "They will have whatever they want in Jannah, and we have something even more than what they will want in Jannah".

What is this additional thing? Those who do good, shall have better than the best. What is better than the best?

Our Prophet SAW explicitly said that, "This gift is the looking at the face of Allah SWT".

Also, in the famous Hadith of Amar Ibn Yasir RA, narrated in the Sunnah Ibn Majah, our Prophet SAW made a beautiful Dua to Allah SWT, "O Allah SWT I ask you for the sweetness of looking at your noble face. And I want to be excited to meet you". It is because the believers will be excited to meet Allah SWT, and the hypocrite and Munafiqun, and the kuffar will be dreading to meet Allah SWT.

Allah SWT mentions in Surah Al Mutaffifin verse 15, "Know that on that day, those people who rejected me, they shall be veiled from their lord. They shall have a veal between me and them". Imam Ash Shafi RA said, "When Allah SWT is going to veil himself from the Kafir, this shows that he shall reveal himself to the Momin". What a beautiful extraction.

Now, Question comes, how can we see Allah SWT when Allah SWT says in the Quran, "You shall not see me". This is something very explicit. Allah SWT says in the Quran, "Eyes cannot see Allah SWT. Eyes cannot encompass Allah SWT and Allah SWT encompasses all eyes". The answer to this is that, these verses are in context. The context is that, in the first one, Musa AS is asking Allah SWT, "Oh Allah let me see you". And Allah SWT said, "O Musa, you cannot see me in this weak and fragile human state. In this state of flesh-and-blood, you cannot see me. And I will demonstrate to you that you cannot see me".

Then Allah SWT displayed himself to the mountain and the mountain fell down completely crumbled and Musa AS fainted because of that. Then Musa AS said, "I seek refuge in you O exalted. I know I cannot see you".

Therefore, when Allah SWT said to Musa AS, "You shall not see me"; this is not a permanent negation. It has indication in the context of the question of Musa AS. Allah SWT cannot be seen by flesh and blood life, the life of this Dunya. Our weak fragile bodies made out of flesh and blood and bones cannot see Allah SWT in this state.

But the state of the Akhira is a different state. In that state, yes indeed the Quran and the Sunnah are very explicit that the believers shall see Allah SWT. As for the second verse that, "Eyes cannot encompass Allah SWT"; our scholars mention that Allah SWT is not negating that he can be seen. Allah SWT is negating that that he can be encompassed or comprehended. It is a higher level than seeing. It means to be fully aware of and to be fully surrounded.

Allah SWT is saying that "Eyes cannot fully surround me. I'm too magnificent for the eye to fully comprehend and understand me". It is a higher level than to simply see with our eyes. This is very explicit in the Quran. Allah

SWT says, "The faces will be shining bright because they will be looking at Allah SWT". This is the believers simply seeing Allah SWT. Even then, after seeing Allah SWT we shall not be able to comprehend Allah SWT.

Hadith of Abu Huraira RA

There are many evidences of the fact that Allah SWT will be seen on the day of judgment. There is a famous Hadith in Sahih Al Bukhari and Sahih Muslim. It is a very beautiful Hadith with so many benefits. It is a very long hadith of Bukhari. It's all about the day of judgment and it is something that is very pertinent.

This Hadith talks about seeing Allah SWT, but it also talks about many other things in the day of judgment. Hadith number is 7437. The Hadith is from Abu Huraira RA. That he asks the Prophet SAW, "O Messenger of Allah SAW, will we see Allah SWT on the day of Judgement?" The Prophet SAW responded, "Does it irritate you? Does it harm you to look at the full moon in the night of the clear sky? And when you look at it it's so beautiful, it's magnificent".

He said, "Oh Messenger of Allah SAW, not at all". The Prophet SAW says, "Are you able to see the sun on a day when there are no clouds?" They said, "Yes indeed O Messenger of Allah SAW". He SAW said, "Then know that you shall see your lord on the day of judgment like you look at the sun and moon. And you will see Allah SWT on the day that Allah SWT gathers all of mankind on the day of judgement. And it will be said that, 'Let everybody follow the icon that used to worship'. Therefore, whoever used to worship the sun will go to the sun. Whoever used to worship the moon will go to the moon. Whoever used to worship the false gods, will go to the false gods. And this Ummah shall remain, because there is no place to go".

Meaning Allah SWT will say or maybe the Angels AS will say that every group should follow the god that they worshipped in Dunya. So, every single group is going to go to its god, whether it was a cross, or an idol etc. They will go looking for their false gods. Then this Ummah shall be left. They will say, "This is where we will remain until our Lord comes to us. When he comes to us, then we will recognize him".

Prophet SAW said, "Allah SWT will come to them in a manner that they will recognize. And Then Allah SWT will say to them, 'I am your lord'. And they will acknowledge, 'Yes indeed you are our Lord'. And then they will follow Allah SWT".

Now, this hadith is summarizing various aspects of the day of judgment. The Hadith is missing few events that will take place after seeing Allah SWT and before the Ummah will follow Allah SWT, like the Hisab etc. but at some point, on the day of judgment, Muslims will follow Allah SWT.

The hadith goes on, "And the bridge is going to be laid in between the two places of Jahannam" And the Prophet SAW said, "Myself and my Ummah shall be the first that is going to cross over the Sirat. Allah SWT will lead the Muslims to a place where then they have to cross over the Sirat. And I (the Prophet SAW) will be the first to cross over the Sirat. And then my Ummah will be the first to follow. And no one shall be speaking at that point in time except for the Prophets AS".

There shall be such dread, such terror, that no one will say a word, other than the Prophets AS. What will the Prophets AS say? "O Allah peace! peace!". Every Prophet AS is going to be asking Allah SWT for security for their Ummah. Hadith continues, "And coming from Jahannam they're going to be hooks, like the thorns from the Trees of As Sa'dan". It's a type of tree that was common in certain areas of Hijaz. These trees have long prickly Thorns.

The Prophet SAW asked the Sahaba if they knew about this tree and they said, "Yes, we know". So, he SAW said, "It will be like those or even bigger. And no one will know its size other than Allah SWT. And it will come from Jahannam and it will drag some people down based upon their deeds. Some people will slip from the Sirat. Some people will be dragged down. And some people will be able to go onwards".

Meaning, this Sirat or the bridge will be over Jahannam and once you cross it, then Jannah is on the other side. But not everybody will cross the Sirat. There will be some people who were Muslims in this world outwardly, but they did not have Iman in their hearts. We seek Allah SWT's refuge. Or there will be some people who were Muslims but their sins were so many, that they don't deserve to enter Jannah immediately.

These people will be taken from the Sirat. Either they will slip themselves. Or there're going to be hooks coming from Jahannam and taking them down. And some people will pass through without any irritation or harm whatsoever.

The Hadith then goes on, "After Allah SWT has finished all of the decrees between the creation, then he will ask the Angels and he will ask the people, that whoever testified La Ilaha Il Allah without Shirk, they can be taken out of Jahannam". Now, this is the Shafa'a that was discussed in the previous book. The concept of Shafa'a of the Prophets AS, the Angels, and the righteous.

They Hadith says, "They shall recognize them by the signs of Sujood. The fire will eat the person except for the place he did Sujood on. Allah SWT has made it haram for the fire to eat the remnants of the Sajda. They will be taken out of Jahannam. Certain groups of these people, they will be charred. They will be burnt to a crisp. They will be poured upon a water that is called the Water of Life. They will flourish under that water. Just like the seed will flourish when there is water pouring over it".

Hadith Continues, "Then (and there's a beautiful a point over here) there will be one person who will be taken out of Jahannam by somebody (either an Angel or a friend or a Prophet AS). And he will be left there outside. His face will be towards Jahannam and he cannot move it anywhere else, because that is his punishment".

The Prophet SAW said, "This is the last person to exit the fire of hell and enter Jannah. And he will exit Jahannam at this stage. His body is outside, but his face is facing Jahannam. He will stay there for as long as Allah SWT wills. Then he will say, 'Oh my Lord, can you please turn my face away from Jahannam, because the heat and the stench of Jahannam is harming me'. So, Allah SWT will say to him, 'O servant of mine, if I give you this, will you be happy? You're not going to ask for anything more are you?' And the servant will say, 'I swear by your honor I will never ask you anything more'. He will continue to promise Allah SWT to never ask anything more. So, Allah SWT allow him to turn his face away from Jahannam".

But when he turns away from Jahannam, he's going to see in the distance far away, Jannah itself. The Prophet SAW said, "He will remain quiet as long as Allah SWT wills him to remain quiet. Then he will say, 'O Allah SWT, allow me to be a little bit closer to Jannah'. Allah SWT will say, 'Didn't you promise me that you would never ask anything more?' And he will say that, 'Oh Allah SWT just this. I promise you, I'll ask nothing more'. Allah SWT will say, 'Do you swear that if I give you this, you won't ask me anything more?' So, he will continue to give Kasam to Allah SWT".

Once he gets closer, the hadith says in Sahih Muslim, "He will be able to hear the laughter of Jannah and he can smell the fragrances of Jannah". The same story keeps on occurring 5 or 10 times. He keeps on coming closer and closer and closer. Until finally, the Hadith in Bukhari says that, "Allah SWT allows him to come to the gates of Jannah".

Now when he gets to the gates of Jannah, he can see inside, and he can see the happiness of the people. He can hear the laughter of the people inside Jannah. Prophet SAW says, "He shall be quiet as long as Allah SWT wills him to be quiet. Then he will say, 'Oh my Lord, cause me to enter Jannah'. So, Allah SWT will say to him, 'Didn't you promise me so many times that you're not going to ask me anything more. Didn't you make Kasam that if I gave it to you, you're not going to ask me. I got your face away from Jahannam and I kept you coming closer and closer to Jannah. Now you want to enter Jannah?' And the man will say, 'Oh my Lord don't make me your most unfortunate creature. That I'm at the gates of Jannah and I'm not inside Jannah'."

The Prophet SAW said, "Allah SWT will laugh at this impetuous man". The purpose here is to demonstrate to us humans and mortals is that we should never say to Allah SWT that we are never going to ask for anything more. Because we need Allah SWT at every single instant. One breath we take, we cannot expel it without the blessings of Allah SWT. We cannot inhale another, without the blessings of Allah SWT. Never ever feel that' if Allah SWT gives me this one thing, then I will need nothing else.

You and your existence, you and your breath, you and your food and water, every time you take, it is from Allah SWT. Do not be so arrogant as to say that you just want this and nothing else. On the contrary say to Allah SWT, "I want everything that you can give me. Because you are the Rab and I am the Abd and Fakir". That's the attitude a person should have.

This person obviously does not have that knowledge. Allah SWT says in the Quran, "Man is so weak that he thinks he can live without the blessings of Allah SWT". This person just wanted his face turned away. Then he keeps on asking to get little bit closer. Every time he gets closer, the smell gets stronger, the laughter gets stronger. He stays quite as long as he can. Then he asks Allah SWT to move him closer. Until finally he gets to the very edge of Jannah. He's at the gates of Jannah. He can see inside Jannah. Then he asks Allah SWT to enter him in Jannah. Then Allah SWT laughs.

Our Prophet SAW said, "As soon as Allah SWT laughs, the man shall enter. Allah SWT laughs at those whom he loves". This man whatever he did, for that he deserved Jahannam. But he still had some good in him. Our Prophet SAW said, "This is the last person exiting Jahannam".

He will enter Jannah. Once he enters it, Allah SWT will say to him, "Go ahead and wish". So, he will ask Allah SWT and ask Allah SWT and ask Allah SWT. Then Allah SWT will remind him of other things to ask. Until when he has been given all that he can possibly imagine, the Prophet SAW said, Allah SWT will say, "You have all that you asked for and 10 times this much".

The man will say, "Oh Allah SWT are you making fun of me? Are you being sarcastic? That I asked and asked. I got out of things to ask. You told me what to ask. I asked for those things. Then you are saying to me, that I will get this and 10 times more?" And when the Prophet SAW said this, he himself began to laugh.

Remember, this is the lowest of the lowest of the lowest person of Jannah that you can you imagine. Can you imagine this man is asking everything his imagination can have and Allah SWT even reminds him of things he doesn't remember? Then Allah says that he will have this and ten times this amount. What do you think the person who is in the middle, or what do you think the person in the highest of the high will get?

This man asked Allah SWT from what his brain could understand. What he had wished for. As for the highest categories of Jannah, our Prophet SAW said, "In that category of Jannah, is that which eyes have never seen. Ears have never heard of. And Minds have never conceived of. We do not even know them. Words cannot describe what is in that category of Jannah". That's the level that I want and all of us should want.

Displaying of Mankind to Allah SWT

Now we are still discussing the very beginnings of the Day of Judgment. We have covered the coming out of the grave. We have covered the Shafa'a, and the fact that our Prophet SAW shall intercede on behalf of all of mankind so that the judgment begins. Then we mentioned the evidences from the Quran and from the Sunnah regarding the fact that Allah Subhanahu WA Ta'ala shall himself come on the day of judgement.

Now, after the coming of Allah Azza Wajal, the next thing that will happen is the displaying of mankind in front of Allah SWT. The fact that all of the creation, the Muslim and the kaffir, the jinn and the inns, all of them will be standing in front of Allah Subhana WA Ta'ala. And Allah Azza WA JAL will look upon, or will gaze upon the creation. This is very explicit in the Quran and in the Sunnah.

The Quran mentions a number of different phrases that display the notion of Allah Subhana WA Ta'ala looking upon the creation. Or to be more precise, the creation being displayed to Allah Subhanahu WA Ta'ala. Of the words that is used in this regard is Uru'da. This word is used in the passive tense. Which basically means 'they shall be displayed'. "They" meaning us. Meaning the creation.

The meaning here is that the Angels will gather up mankind. Or that mankind themselves will be gathered in a way that Allah Subhana WA Ta'ala knows how. Allah Azza WA JAL will then come and we shall be displayed in front of Allah Subhanahu WA Ta'ala.

The evidences for this are plenty. Of them, three verses in the Quran in order of their chronology, Surah Hud verse 18, Allah SWT says, "Who does more injustice than the one who lies against Allah SWT? These people, they shall be displayed in front of their Lord. And the witnesses will point out that these are the people who lied about Allah Subhanahu Wa'ta'ala. Verily Allah SWT's Lana is upon those who have done injustice. And the height of injustice, the worst injustice, even worse than Shirk, is to lie against Allah SWT. To say about Allah SWT, something that Allah SWT did not say".

In this verse, we see that on the day of judgement there shall be the Angels as witnesses, who will be pinpointing out groups of people. This will happen when all of mankind is standing in front of Allah SWT. Angels will then testify that these are the liars who have lied against Allah SWT.

In Surah Al-Kahf verse 48, Allah SWT says, "And they shall all be displayed in front of their Lord in rows and ranks". Imagine all of mankind being gathered together. Subhan Allah, when we look at gatherings that are done in these places that have 10,000 people. Can you imagine hundreds of millions? Can you imagine many, many billions of people, all lined up in straight rows?

All of mankind that ever existed shall be gathered and presented in front of Allah SWT. But even though we are in rows, with billions and billions of people around us, we shall feel alone in front of Allah Subhana WA Ta'ala. As Allah SWT says in the Quran, "When you have come to us like we created you the first time, you have come to us one-on-one".

So even though there will be millions and billions of people around us, When Allah SWT comes, the feeling will be that we are all alone. We are standing in front of Allah SWT. As Allah SWT says, "When you have come back to us like we created you the first time around". What is the reference here for "Like we created you the first time around"?

There are a number of interpretations. Of the interpretations is that, this is not the first time we were standing in front of Allah Subhana WA Ta'ala. Rather we have stood in front of Allah SWT before this point in time. But at that point in time, we didn't have physical bodies. We only had our souls. Allah Azza WA JAL mentions in the Quran very explicitly, as the Prophet SAW explained this verse, "All of the souls were gathered in front of Allah SWT, and Allah SWT spoke to all of them directly, and Allah SWT asked them, 'Am I not your Lord?'"

When did that happened? It happened at the beginning of the creation. When Allah SWT created the creation. Meaning with the creation the souls. All of our souls were created simultaneously at one point in time, other than the soul of Adam AS and Hawwa RA. These two were created before us. First our parents were created. Then at one point in time, all of the children of Adam AS, from the time of Adam AS' children, up until the day of judgment; their souls were simultaneously created.

Now, on the day of judgement, all of the souls are resurrected. That is why Allah SWT says, "Just like we did it once before, you have come back to us once again". Subhan Allah, in the twinkling of an eye, from the beginning of the creation, to the end of the creation. That's one interpretation.

The other interpretation is that, when Allah SWT says, "You have come back to us the way we created you", means, 'You have nothing other than what we gave you. You have no clothes, no money, no status, no rank, nothing. You are naked, barefoot, and uncircumcised. literally the way you were born, that is the way you have come back'. Both of these interpretations are valid.

Then in Surah Al-Kahf, Allah Subhana WA Ta'ala mentions the display of mankind on the Ard. Then the other verse in the Quran that mentions Ard is Surah Al-Haqqah verse 18. Allah SWT says, "On that day (the day of judgment), all of you shall be displayed in front of Allah Subhana WA Ta'ala. Nothing that you wanted to hide is going to remain hidden on that day".

All of these three verses they mentioned the notion of that we shall be displayed to Allah SWT. This display is for the entire creation, whether you want it or not. Now, there's another series of verses, with another verb, which also indicates that all of us will be displayed in front of Allah SWT.

This other word that is used in the Quran is Baraza. Barraza means to show without any hindrance, without any veil. That means it's out in the open. That means nothing is covering you. There's no shade. It means that everyone will be clear and apparent. There's nothing blocking them. This is another term that is used multiple times in the Quran.

For example, in Surah Ibrahim verse 21 Allah Subhana WA Ta'ala says, "And all of them are shown in front of Allah SWT. All of them, with no exception. Every single creation of Allah SWT". Now how long will this display last? We do not know. How many eons, or centuries, or thousands of years, we do not know.

However, we can derive from the generality of other text that for the believers this will be zoomed on. For the believers, it's going to be a moment of honor and pleasure. For the opposite, it is going to be a moment of dishonor and terror.

Allah SWT continues, "All of them will be displayed to Allah SWT. Those who were weak and oppressed, those who were the sheep following the leaders, they would say to those who they were following, (the arrogant people), 'We only obeyed you. You told us to worship these false gods. You told us to kill and to plunder (meaning the military that's plundering). It's not our fault. You told us to kill those innocent people, and we killed them. We only followed you. Are you now going to take your share of the punishment? Are you going to help us and defend that we just followed your orders?'. The leaders will say, 'It's not our fault that you only followed us. We're all in this together'. And they're not going to take their share of the blame".

Another verse of Surah Ibrahim, verse 48, Allah SWT says, "On that day, the day that the earth shall be substituted for another earth, and the skies shall be substituted for other skies, all of them are going to be shown in front of Allah SWT. The one. The single. Everyone else is in front of Allah SWT. And the Wahid is the one who will look upon them. He is the one who overpowers and the one who conquers".

In Surah Ghafir verse 16, once again the same names of Allah SWT come. Allah SWT says, "On that day, all of them shall be displayed without any protection. There will be nothing to conceal them. There is not going to be a tree or anything else. Everything will be flat, and they'll be standing in rows. On that day, they will be in front of Allah SWT displayed. Nothing will be hidden in front of Allah SWT. Allah SWT will know everything".

Then Allah SWT will say, "To whom does the kingdom belong?" Then Allah SWT will answer, "To Allah, the Wahid and the Qahhar".

In Surah Al-Kahf as well, we have the same notion, Allah SWT says, "On that day, the earth is going to be clear. No veil is going to cover the earth. Not a single person is left when we gather all of them". It is as if Allah SWT is saying that there is nothing that is going to cover mankind. All of mankind will be in front of Allah SWT. And will be displayed and shown to Allah SWT.

In the hadith in Sahih Muslim, narrated by Jarir Ibn Abdullah RA, that the Prophet SAW said, "Verily the Ard is not just for the kafir or for the Muslim, it is for the creation without any exception. Pay attention to the fact, I'm making it very clear, all of you will be displayed in front of your Lord. And you will see him as you are seeing this full moon". Then Prophet SAW pointed to the full moon that was there in the middle of the month.

Now this shows us that the coming of Allah SWT and the seeing of Allah SWT and the display of mankind, they are in fact the same thing. That when Allah Azza Wajal comes down with the angels, that will be for this display of mankind. So, in the same manner, as we today can see the moon in the sky, we are going to see Allah Subhana WA Ta'ala on that day.

Number of times Mankind will be displayed

Now, how many times shall this display take place? There is one tradition that actually mentions that this will occur more than once. The Quran does not mention quantity. There's one hadith that does mention the number of times.

This hadith is found in Musnad Imam Ahmed, which is the largest existent book of hadith. There is no book of hadith that is larger than Musnad Imam Ahmed. It has 50 volumes. Imam Muhammad was also the teacher of Imam Bukhari. The Hadith relevant to us is in volume 32 page 486. Now, Musnad Imam Ahmed is arranged not according to topics, like Sahih Bukhari and Sahih Muslim are. It is arranged according to Sahabah narrating the Hadith. Meaning all of the narrations of Abu Bakr Siddiq RA are in one section. Then the narrations of Umar RA are in the next section, etc.

The Hadith we are discussing is narrated by Abu Musa Al-Ashari RA. Hadith number is 19,715. The Prophet SAW said, "People will be displayed on the day of judgment in three displays. People will be displayed three times. As for the first two, it will be defenses and excuses".

Meaning, you will be challenged, then you will have a time to defend yourself. You will be presented with your accusations and then you will have a chance to defend yourself.

Hadith continues, "Then as for the third display, that will be the time that the scrolls will then be given and the result will be handed back. Some people will hold it with the right hand (May Allah SWT make us amongst them) and others will hold with the left hand (we seek refuge from being amongst them)".

This is explicit in the Quran that, "Some people will get the results in the right hand. And some will get them in the left hand, and out of shame, they will put them behind their back".

This hadith explicitly mentions there shall be three times that we're going to have this dialogue with Allah SWT, and Allah Azza WA JAL will speak directly to us. This hadith is also found with a similar chain in Tirmidhi. But this one has more details in the wording.

However, some scholars have pointed out that this hadith has a missing link in its chain between Hasan al-Basri RA and Abu Musa Al-Ashari RA. It has a very slight weakness to it. It is really one of the slightest weaknesses possible. Nonetheless, this narration is not Sahih or authentic narration. It is a beautiful narration, but we should simply add the caveat that Allah Subhanahu WA Ta'ala knows best.

A Private Meeting

There are other evidences in the Quran and, in the Sunnah, that Allah Subhana wa Ta'ala is going to see all of us or meet all of us. This other genre of evidences deals with another term that has a more specific connotation, which means a private meeting, or meeting face to face.

Allah Subhana WA Ta'ala mentions this concept of in the Quran in almost a dozen verses. In Surah al-An'am verse 94, Allah Subhana WA Ta'ala says, "You have come to us **individually, one by one**". So, each one of us will be in front of Allah SWT one by one.

Allah Subhana WA Ta'ala mentions, "The believers are those who, they are certain that they're going to **meet** their Lord". The word used for **meet** means 'in a one-on-one meeting'.

In the Quran Allah SWT also says, "Whoever is desiring to meet his lord, know that you're going to meet Allah Subhana WA Ta'ala".

In the Quran as well, "Fear Allah SWT and be certain that you're going to meet Allah Subhana WA Ta'ala".

In Surah Al-Inshiqaq Allah SWT says, "O mankind you are laboring very intensely towards your Lord (meaning we are continually doing our deeds whether they're good or they're bad), and you are going to meet Allah

SWT". So very clearly in the Quran we have this notion of a private meeting with Allah Subhana WA Ta'ala.

There's also a very beautiful hadith narrated by Ibn Abbas RA about Allah SWT covering up his servant and speaking to him one on one that says, "There shall not be any interpreter between him and the person". Once again, a very explicit affirmation of a meeting.

Now, how can Allah Subhana WA Ta'ala speak to all of us individually, when we are in the billions? The first to ask this question was the cousin of the Prophet SAW, Ibn Abbas RA. Somebody asked Ibn Abbas RA, "O Ibn Abbas, how will Allah Subhana WA Ta'ala speak to all of us individually, simultaneously?" Ibn Abbas RA said, "The same way Allah SWT provides all of them their Rizq simultaneously".

Now does this individual meeting takes place at the very beginning of the display or is that going to take place later on? We do not know. The text does not indicate that it is going to be right then and there, or is it going to be later on.

Understand that the chronology of events on the day of judgment is something that is not 100% known to us for multiple reasons. Therefore, will Allah Subhana WA Ta'ala speak to in us individually at the very beginning when he comes or will that be delayed for a later time;

we do not know. It is possible that it will be immediate and it is possible that will be done afterwards.

Allah Subhana WA Ta'ala says in the Quran in Surah Nuh, "Those who don't believe in Allah SWT, those who are Kuffar, their good deeds are like mirages in the desert. But they are not going to find anything". Meaning here is that they think they have good deeds, and they will rush to go find their good deeds on the day of judgment. But they will not find anything as they haven't done good deeds.

Then Allah SWT says, "Rather than finding your illusory good deeds, rather than finding this illusion and mirage, he shall find Allah SWT in front of him. He shall find Allah SWT right there. And Allah SWT will then deal with his judgement and make the Hisab of him right then. And how fast is Allah SWT in Hisab". This verse is very explicit.

When Allah Subhana wa Ta'ala comes, and when the believers will see Allah SWT, this will be the first time they will see Allah SWT. But this isn't the only time we will see Allah SWT. The believers will see Allah SWT multiple times. They will see him on the day of judgment and then they shall see him again in Jannah. May Allah SWT make us amongst those people.

The seeing of Allah SWT on the Day of Judgment is not the same as the seeing of Allah SWT in Jannah. The seeing on Allah SWT on the day of judgment is indeed a blessing and it is indeed a reward and a gift. But the seeing of Allah SWT in Jannah is a much higher blessing in a way we don't understand.

There is nothing in Jannah that is higher than the blessing of gazing upon the face of Allah Subhanahu Wa'ta'ala. That blessing is for to the people of Jannah, after the enter Jannah. As for Qiyamah, it is going to be a glimpse of that blessing.

Who Will See Allah SWT?

Now, who will see Allah SWT? the believers only? Or all of mankind, including those who rejected Allah SWT? For this issue there is nothing that is definitive. That will those who rejected Allah SWT also see Allah SWT on the day of judgment.

There is unanimous consensus that the blessing of seeing Allah SWT is the highest blessing that is going to be given to all the righteous believers who enter Jannah. But the question is; on the day of judgment, will the kafir see Allah SWT or not? Ibn Taymiyyah RA was asked about this and he wrote an entire treatise on this.

He says that this is a debate that was unknown in the time of the Sahaba. He mentions that there are three opinions about this issue. He says that the majority position is that the kafir will not see Allah SWT on the Day of Judgement. Allah SWT will see them. They will not see Allah SWT. Allah SWT will see the kaffir because Allah SWT will look at all the creation when they are displayed in front of him.

He then quotes the verse in the Quran, "Verily on that day, there shall be a veil between them and Allah Subhanahu Wa'ta'ala". He then says that Imam Malik RA was also asked this question. Imam Malik replied, "The kafir does not see Allah SWT (based upon the above verse). The whole purpose of this verse therefore is that the believers will see Allah SWT".

Imam As-Shafi RA was asked about this verse and he also said the same thing that, "When Allah SWT has taken a veil for the Kafir, this shows that his chosen servants shall have no veil, and they shall see Allah SWT". So, the first position is that the kafir will never see Allah SWT.

The second position is that the kafir will see Allah SWT, but it will not be same as the seeing of the Momin. The kafir will see Allah SWT, but it will be a seeing of terror and fear. Not a seeing of comfort and honor. Allah SWT will display himself to the believers in a manner that will give them comfort, in a manner that will give them hope, in a manner that will increase their Iman.

As for the kaffir, their seeing of Allah SWT will only increase them in terror and in fright. Just like a criminal is brought forth in front of the judge and the criminal knows he's guilty and the criminal knows he's going to be sentenced. And the judge or the ruler, when the criminal is brought in front of, that is not an honor. It is a dishonor. And the person is terrified.

This is driven from the generalities of the verses that, "All of you will see him". And that, "There is no single person except that Allah SWT will speak to him". And, "There's no intermediary between them". So, the generality of the Quran and Sunnah might seem to indicate as well that the kafir will see Allah SWT.

Then the third position is that, the kafir will not see Allah SWT. But the Mumin, and the hypocrite, and some of the people of the book will see Allah SWT. The people of the book are highest category amongst the non-Muslims. Especially the righteous amongst them, those who did not hear of Islam and they lived righteous lives will see Allah SWT.

Allah SWT says in the Quran that, "There are some of the people of the book, when they listen to the Quran, they are crying out of love and fear of Allah Subhanahu Wa'ta'ala". Now, according to the third opinion the hypocrite will be taken away and will end up in Jahannam.

Ibn Tamia said was sympathetic to the first opinion which is that only the believers will see Allah SWT, and those who rejected Allah SWT will not see him on the day of judgement.

Allah SWT Speaking to Mankind

Again, I reiterate that all of the aspects being discussed are not necessarily in chronological order. Rather any one of these can occur at any point on the day of judgement. For the actual sequence of events, we do not have an exact idea, but rather a generic one. And we are going roughly in the generic idea.

But one of the key points is that, it does appear that the day of Judgment's events are going to be relative for each person. Each person is going to face slightly different scenarios. And their time frame will also be different from person to person.

Now, we move on to the issue of issue of Allah SWT speaking to the creation and the creation hearing the speech of Allah SWT. This is something that is very explicit in both the Quran and in the Sunnah.

Allah SWT mentions in Surah Al-A'raf verse 6 to 7, "We will ask those who were sent a Prophet, and we will ask the Prophets AS themselves". It is a part of the reckoning. And Allah SWT would begin by talking to the Prophets AS.

This is mentioned a number of verses. Of them, is Surah Maida verse 109. Allah SWT says that, "On the day that

Allah SWT will gather all of the Prophets AS; Allah SWT will ask them, 'what was the response of your people?'".

With regards to the specific questioning of mankind, Allah SWT mention is Surah Al-Hijr verse 92 to 93, "By your lord, we are going to ask each and every one of them what they used to do". Meaning Allah SWT is swearing on himself that he will question all of us without any exception.

There are a number of Hadiths in this genre as well. Of them is a beautiful Hadith in Bukhari. It is the famous Hadith of Abdullah Ibn Unais RA, in which he said that, he heard the Prophet SAW say that, "Allah SWT will gather of all of mankind on the day of Judgment. They will be naked. They will be barefoot. They will be uncircumcised. The way that their mothers gave birth to them. He will then shout out to them and address them with a loud voice. The one who is far away will hear it in the same manner as the one who was nearby. Then Allah SWT will say, 'I am the king and I am the one who shall be the ultimate judge. All subjugate themselves to me'. Everyone will hear Allah SWT's reckoning and Allah SWT's statement regarding himself".

The Prophet SAW mentioned in a number of Hadiths that Allah SWT will speak to Adam AS, and Allah SWT will speak to Nuh AS, and Allah SWT will speak to Ibrahim AS, and Allah SWT will speak to the Prophet

Muhammad SAW. This speech will be to the Prophets AS and then Allah SWT will also speak to the believers.

Ask for those who rejected Allah SWT, there are some evidences that says that Allah SWT will speak to them, and there are other evidences that says that Allah SWT will not speak to them.

For example, there is the phrase that is very common in the Quran that, "Allah SWT will not speak to them, and Allah SWT will not look at them, and Allah STW will not purify them". Allah SWT also says in the Quran, "Be quit, and do not speak to me".

In the Hadith in Sahih Bukhari, the Prophet SAW said, "3 are the people that Allah SWT will not look at them, and Allah will not speak to them, and Allah SWT will not purify them. Of them is the one who is arrogant and the one who is using Allah SWT's name in vain".

But there are other versus, that we here and we get the impression that all of the creation of Allah SWT will hear the voice of Allah SWT. Ibn Kathir RA comments on these two genres of evidence. He says that, this means that Allah SWT will not look to them with a look of mercy, and Allah will not speak to them with a speech of mercy.

Because the other evidence is that, all of mankind will be in front of Allah SWT, and he will look upon all of mankind. Yet, there are going to be some people who he looks at with the look of his mercy. And those who rejected Allah SWT, they will not be given that look.

Also, regarding issue of Allah SWT not speaking to disbelievers, Al Qurtubi RA and others, they comment that the day of judgment is very long, and speech of Allah SWT for the one who rejects Allah SWT, will be a punishment, and at times the Silence of Allah SWT will be a punishment. Both of them will be a punishment for those who rejected Allah SWT.

To understand, imagine that some people are taken to jail and they cannot even speak to the judge. They cannot even speak to a court of law. That cutting off of communication is a type of torture for them. Then imagine if they are brought in front of a judge, and the only purpose is so that this person is sentenced and punished. Then that communication itself is the punishment for them.

This is a worldly example not in order to compare that to Allah SWT, but to compare the situation that we might understand in this world and then extrapolate it to the next world. When such a person is not spoken to and is in solitary confinement, that is a torture. And when he is brought in front of a tribunal that has already decided his fate, and that he's guilty, that too is a torture.

Therefore, we can reconcile that at certain time frames Allah SWT will not speak and will not allow them to speak, and that is a punishment to them. In other time frames, Allah SWT will speak to them and that speaking itself is going to be the height of terror. Because when Allah SWT is going to point out to you your own sins, and you know that they are true; imagine how terrified that is going to feel.

Mechanisms of Hisab

Now, we get to issue of the actual Hisab, or the actual reckoning. When we say Hisab, we mean the actual reckoning, that is going to happen line by line. It will be done in multiple ways and batches. It is going to be in multiple mechanism.

One of the mechanisms of Hisab and the one that we want, is what is called Al Ard. We already mentioned this in previous chapter. That is simply the overall examination and selection. That Allah SWT will look upon the entire creation and for some people that in and of itself is the Hisab. Every one of us will have a private moment with Allah SWT.

That private moment, even though we're all surrounded by billions and billions of people at that point in time, it will be as if we are alone. As if Allah SWT is focusing every attention on us. That's going to be our perception.

Ibn Abbas RA was asked, "How will Allah do the Hisab of all of mankind simultaneously?" Ibn Abbas RA responded, "The same way that he provides them their sustenance simultaneously. Allah SWT is taking care of all of our sustenance simultaneously. Why can't he take care of all of our reckoning simultaneously as well?"

Generic Presentation

So, the one of the mechanisms of this Reckoning, and it is going to be the lightest, and it is going to be the stage that is the least difficult, and it is the stage that we want. That is the stage of the Ard or the generic presentation.

The notion of a generic presentation is mentioned explicitly in the Hadith of Bukhari narrated by our mother Aisha RA. She stated that, once the Prophet SAW said that, "Whoever is going to be questioned and whoever is going to be examined, that is going to be a punishment".

So, Aisha RA said, "Ya Rasool Allah SAW, doesn't Allah SWT say in the Quran that there are going to be people that will have an easy Hisab? How can it be a punishment, when Allah SWT is saying that it's going to be an easy Hisab?"

The Prophet SAW said that, "That what you're talking about in the verse is the presentation. It is not a defense. It is not an examination". Therefore, an easy Hisab or presentation or Al Ard means that Allah SWT will not go in to details of a person's deeds. But for those whose entire list of deeds is questioned one by one, that is going to be the detailed examination and accounting and a punishment in itself.

So, when Allah SWT says in the Quran, "He will be accounted for with an easy accounting"; that's what we want. And for the one who will have his deeds checked line by line, even if he passes, it will be a sort of punishment for him. Here we should note that, going line by line does not mean he's going to go to Jahannam.

For example, imagine on your tax forms, even if you did everything correctly, and the government sends you a mail or a message that they want receipts, or evidence, or they want to check that every single line of your tax forms is accurate; even if you did everything accurately, for you to be under government scrutiny, will feel like a type of punishment.

This is what the Prophet SAW is saying that if Allah SWT is going to ask you for every single point, and even if you pass, that will feel like a type of punishment, that you don't want. Now, the highest level of Iman will not get that. Detailed Hisab is going to be those that their good and bad deeds are struggling with one another. Or people who are worse than this.

The Scroll of Deeds

Another concept of Hisab that we need to understand is that, there will actually be physical evidence presented in the courts of law on that day of judgement. There will be an exhibit of evidences. What is that ultimate exhibit? What is that main proof of evidence that will be brought forth?

The main point of evidence is going to be the scroll of deeds, that has our own actions written down by the Angels. This notion of our scrolls and the notion of our own deeds being presented back to us, is a central motif of the day of judgment.

There are more than two dozen evidence is in the Quran and Sunnah combined, that mention that we will be getting back scrolls of our deeds that we ourselves have done, on the day of judgment.

In Arabic the word scroll means rolled up and opened up. Allah SWT mentions this concept in the Quran, that our good deeds are being written down, and this is something that every single one of us knows. We hear about it since we are children. That we have Angels that are recording each and every deed of ours.

Angels Recording the Deeds

Allah SWT says in the Quran that, "On his right and on his left, they are sitting down. Not the single word does he say except that it has an observant and a guardian". Allah SWT is describing the two Angels that are constantly writing down what we have done and making sure that nothing slips by.

In Surah Al-Infitar Allah SWT says, "Indeed you have those that are protecting you. They are noble writers. They know exactly what you have done". So, they're writing down the deeds that you have done.

In Surah Al Imran verse 181 Allah SWT challenges those who have done wrong, and Allah SWT says to them, "We are writing down what they have said".

In Surah Yasin, in the famous verse, in the first page of Surah Yasin, Allah SWT says, "We shall indeed resurrect the dead and we are writing down all that they have done to send forward, their good Deeds and their bad deeds. And we are writing down even their footsteps".

In other words, that book is so comprehensive that nothing shall be escaping from it, including every step that you have taken. Then Allah SWT continues, "And every little thing that they have done we have preserved it in the original registrar".

In Surah Tawbah verse 120 to 121, Allah SWT says that, "It is not appropriate for the people of Medina and for the Bedouins around the city of Medina, that they stay behind when the Prophet SAW goes out. And that they don't prefer themselves over him. That is because whenever they become thirsty, whenever they become tired, whenever they become hungry in the way of Allah SWT; whenever they take one step in the way of Allah SWT to enrage those who reject Allah SWT; whenever they do anything against an enemy; except that it should be written down for them".

Parenthetically, it is not just two Angels. Indeed, two Angels are assigned no doubt. But there are more than two Angels that are writing things down. And on the day of judgment it is not just going to be just the two Angels that will be showing our deeds. It will be multiple Angels that have written our deeds. The author will be us via the ink of the Angels. When we see that book, we will know we are the author. We will know we are the ones who wrote that via the medium of various Angels.

There other evidences for it. The Hadith in Sahih Bukhari that our Prophet SAW said that, "On the day of Jumma, the Angels they stand outside the door, and they write down the names of the people in order that they come in. The one who comes in early, will get the more reward". So, there are other Angels that are writing down good deed.

In another hadith in Sahih Bukhari, the Prophet SAW once prayed salah, and when he stood up to the Ruku, he said, "Allah hears the one who praises him". A man heard this, and he instinctively said, "All praises are for Allah SWT". When the Salah finished, the Prophet SAW asked, "Who said that?" There was silence. Then he repeated, "Who said that?"

Then the man sheepishly said, "Ya Rasool Allah SAW, I did and I didn't mean anything wrong. I was just trying to praise Allah SWT". The Prophet SAW said, "Verily I saw more than 30 Angels racing to see who writes it first and takes it back to Allah SWT".

In other words, the phrase that the Sahabi said was so beautiful, that all of the Angels, they were in a competition of who's going to finish writing down and who's going to take it back to Allah SWT. These 30 Angels are not just the Angels that are assigned to us. Indeed, we have Angels that are assigned to us. Our Prophet SAW mentioned this, "The Angels take shifts with you".

It is because they worship Allah SWT in different ways and a part of their worship is to write down our good and bad deeds. And those shifts change at Salat of Fajr and Salat of Asr. If we're praying those two Salah regularly, the Angels will report good news back to Allah SWT.

Authors of Our Scrolls

We should really humble ourselves in front of Allah SWT for so many blessings, and of those blessings is that the Prophet SAW said, hadith is in Musnad Imam Ahmed, that Allah SWT has said, "Allah SWT has written down all of the good deeds and the bad deeds. Whoever sincerely desires to do one good deed, even if he doesn't do it, Allah SWT writes for him a good deal, fully and completely. And if he manages than to actually do it, then Allah SWT will write for him between 10 to 700 times the reward of that one good deed that he did. And whoever desires to do an evil deed, but he does not end up doing it, then Allah SWT will write for him a good deed".

Meaning if you thought of a bad deed, and you said, 'No and I'm not going to do. I fear Allah SWT'. The person changes his mind. The mere fact that he changed his mind. He's sitting and doing nothing. The thought of stealing something came to him. And he goes, "No, I'm not going to steal". Just because he fought an internal desire and he's sitting doing nothing, Allah SWT writes for him good deed.

Then the Prophet SAW said, "And if he ends up doing that evil deed, then he shall get the evil of 1 deed". Subhan Allah! our book is not proportionate. Everything is stacked in the favor of good deeds.

If you desire to do a good deed, then you changed your mind for whatever reason, still you get some reward. If you ended up doing the good deed, you will get from 10 to 700 times the reward. If you desire to do an evil deed, and you changed your mind for the fear of Allah SWT, you will still get a reward. Three of the four times, it is in our favor. Only when you actually ended up doing an evil deed, you get written 1 evil deed.

So, this book is not a fair book, in accordance with the fairness of this world. It is a merciful book, that only the most merciful could right for us. It is a book that we could not even right for ourselves. It is a book that is stacked in our favor. So, woo to the one who is not able to take advantage of the mercy and the blessings of Allah SWT.

We learn that we are writing these books, and these books will then be returned to us. And they will be unfolded in front of us. We will be shown our own books that we have authored.

Imam At-Tabari RA comments on this and he says that, "That is the date when the Scrolls of our good and bad deeds that were rolled up because of our death; they will be opened up, since they have been closed at the time of our death. Come day of judgment, they are going to be opened up and we will see the deeds that were written down, both the good and the bad".

Of the most famous verses in the Quran that really demonstrate that we are the ones that have authored this book and we will get our own book back, and we will see it published in front of us, and we will see it in its pristine and fresh form on the day of judgement, is that Allah says in Surah Isra verse number 14 and 15, "Every person we have attached his decree. On the day of judgement, we will take out for him a book. He's going to find this book spread in front of him. Read your own book. Sufficient is you yourself to be your own judge on the day of judgment".

This is again reiterated in Surah Kahf verse 49, "The book shall be brought out. The Sinners and the criminals will be terrified of this own book, that they see in it. What they see will terrify them. And they will say to us, what type of book is this? Neither a small nor a large deed is left. Everything is recorded in it. All that they themselves have done; they will find it in front of them".

The purpose here is exactly as Allah SWT says, "You will be your own witness against yourself". You will testify against yourself.

This is mentioned in a Hadith is Sunnah Abu Dawood that the Prophet SAW once laughed and Anas RA said, "Ya Rasool Allah SAW, why are you laughing?" So, he said to them, "Do you know why I'm laughing? I am laughing from the speech of Allah SWT with his servant".

On the day of judgment, the servant will say that, "Oh my Lord didn't you promise me that you will not be unjust?" Allah SWT will say, "I did indeed promise". The servants will say, "So then today I will not allow anyone other than myself to testify in my case. I'm not accepting anybody".

The point here is that in the court of law if there is conflict of interest, or a witness is not a neutral, or witness is not credible or trustworthy, their testimony is thrown out. In same sense this person is saying to Allah SWT, 'I don't trust any other human being'. Meaning he's going to try to get out of any witnesses, and he's going to say, 'Let me testify about myself. I'm not going to allow any external testimonies. I'm only going to accept myself as a witness'.

Then Allah SWT will say, "Today you alone will be a witness against yourself". Then the books will be brought that the Kiraman Katibin have written. Then his mouth would be sealed and his body will speak, and the book is going to testify. His mouth will be allowed to speak. The mouth will rebuke his own body, and it will say, "All that I did, I did it for you. All the sins that I did, we did it for each other". But of course, it will be too late for all of that.

This beautiful narration indicates that the purpose of these books being given back to us is that no one can accuse Allah SWT of any Injustice. Remember these detailed line by line examination will not take place for the righteous.

No One will Remember Anyone Else

Once the Prophet SAW returned back to his house and our mother Aisha RA was there and she was crying and the Prophet SAW said, "What is causing you to cry?" Aisha RA said, "I am scared of Jahannam. Will you remember your family on that day? Will you remember all of us on that day?"

The Prophet SAW said, "3 times no one will remember anyone else. The first of them is when the Mizan is brought forth and everyone will be busy in his own thoughts, until he knows whether it will be heavy or light. Second of them is when the book is brought out and it will be said, come read your own book. And a person will be in complete absorbing; and no one will think of anybody else, until the person knows whether he will be given his book from his right or from his left or from behind. Then the third time when no one would remember anybody else is when the bridge is placed over Jahannam and people are told to cross the bridge".

This hadith is a very powerful one, that none of humanity including the Prophet SAW will think of anybody else on these 3 occasions. Of course, he said this as a type of exaggeration. As the Prophets AS and especially our Prophet SAW shall be thinking of his Ummah at all of these times.

Sign of Success or Failure

Also, when these scrolls will be brought out, it will have to be examined, and then we can defend ourselves, and then the verdict will be given.

First this book will be the evidence and then we will have a look at the evidence, then Allah SWT will allow the opportunity for us to defend ourselves, and we will admit that this is what we have done, and then the actual verdict will be handed back to us physically in form of our scrolls.

Now, how they are given to us, will be either the diploma of passing or the stigma of failure. How we pick up our own deeds, and how we return to our families, will already tell us our results. This is something that is very clear in the Quran and in the Sunnah.

Allah SWT mentions in the Surah Al Haqqah and also in Surah Al Infitar that, "On that day 8 of the Angels will carry the throne of Allah SWT, and the whole arena of the day of judgment will be surrounded by Angels and the Throne. On that day, you will be exposed. Nothing should be hidden from you. On that day, Allah SWT will be able to see everything. You will not be able to hide anything. Allah SWT will gaze at everyone".

Then Allah SW mentions, "As for the one who is given his book in the right hand, he's going to be shouting with joy. Then that man will say, 'I knew that I would meet my Hisab on this day. That a day would come when I would meet this actual judgment and my book is going to be returned to me'."

Allah SWT says about this person that, "He shall have a pleasant living in a lofty garden. Its picking and its fruits are easy to reach. Eat and drink merrily, for all of the deeds that you did in the days gone by". Meaning, 'your life that you lived, the difficult life, don't worry about it. Now you should have an easy life'.

As for those who took their book in the left hand, he shall say, "Oh how I wish I had never been given my book back to me. And I don't know what my fate is going to. How I wish that this had never happened. How I wish that I never knew what this account was. If this was all ended and over and non-existent, and I as extinguished. My money is of no use to me. My power is completely destroyed".

Then to these people, Allah SW will say, "Take him. Shackle him. Scorch him. Throw him in the blaze and then chain him to a chain whose length is 70 cubits long. This person, neither did he believe in Allah SWT, nor did he encourage the feeding of the poor. This day he shall have no friend and his food shall be nothing, other than the filth of Jahannam".

This section of versus are very powerful section that describes in vivid detail the issue of the returning of the books and the reaction of those who get their books in the right hand versus those who get their books in the left hand. The one who will get the books back, he will automatically know and only one of his hands will be active.

If he raises the right hand to take the book back, may Allah SWT make us amongst them, that will be the person who passes. The other one who raises from the left hand, he knows that he has failed the exam.

In Surah Al-Inshiqaq verses 6-15 Allah SWT says, "O mankind you are indeed toiling to your Lord. You are laboring towards your lord bit-by-bit, journey by Journey, day by day, trial by trial. You are going to meet him individually. As for him who is given his book in the right hand, he shall get an easy Hisab. And he will return back to his family in a state of happiness".

Now scholars have mentioned that not everybody who gets their book in their right hand, will necessarily have a very easy Hisab. It is possible that the Muslims that are struggling, they might enter Jannah, but on the day of judgment they might be punished lightly by having to go through each and every step of the way of Hisab.

Then Allah SWT says, "As for the one who is given his book behind the back, then he shall indeed call for his own death. And he shall enter the blaze of Jahannam. He used to be arrogant in his own family. He thought he would never come back to Allah SWT. Indeed, Allah SWT was always watching".

Now, it is a common mistake that people make that one must give up all the pleasures of this world to be righteous. And to obtain the pleasures of this world, one must be unrighteous. No. The one who chooses Allah SWT will find the purest of pleasures in this world and he will find the pleasure in the worship of Allah SWT, which is the ultimate pleasure.

The one who chooses the pleasures of this world, will never ever be fully satiated. Forever chasing the pleasures that he wants, forever digging himself deeper into his own bottomless and deepest desires. He's never going to be satisfied until death comes to him. Then he meets Allah SWT and all the happiness that he had in this world will not make him happy in the hereafter.

Behind Their Back

The next point in this series of versus, Allah SWT mentions of the person who will get the book from behind him. Some of our Scholars have said that, there are three categories of people.

The righteous will get it in the right hand. The Sinners going to Jahannam will get it in the left hand. Then the worst of the worst, and they're also going to Jahannam, but they will get it behind their back.

Other scholars have said that when they get it in the left hand, they will be so embarrassed and mortified, that they will attempt to hide their scroll by putting it behind their back.

Protected in Grave

Hasan Al Basri RA said, "O son of Adam, Allah SWT has spread out your own parchment and put in charge of you two Noble Angels. One on your right and the other on your left. So, do as you please and increase or decrease what is written down. When you die, your scroll will be rolled up and placed on your neck in your own grave. Then when you come out of the grave, you will see your own scroll and receive it opened up. So read your own book. For by Allah, whoever has placed you to be your own judge, has shown infinite justice".

This is Al Hasan Al-Basri RA extracting the scenario from the Quran and from the Sunnah, that you're scroll will be put up and tied up and then put on your neck. When you go to your grave, there's going to be a symbolic book or scroll that you have with you.

You're going to literally be protecting it and nobody can tamper with it. Then on the day of judgement you're going to come out and you will open up your own Scrolls to see what you have done.

Different Types of Scrolls

We also learn from the Hadith that not all of these scrolls are of the same length. In one Hadith in Sunnah Ibn Maja, the phrase occurs that the Prophet SAW said that, Allah SWT will say that, "unfold the scrolls".

So, his scrolls will be unrolled out. In one hadith it says, he will have 99 Scrolls. Each one of them, will be as far as the eyes can see. Not every scroll will be the same. Depending on how long you live, and what you did, and the quantity and quality of your deeds, the length of your scrolls will also be different.

There will be different types of scrolls as well. That not all of the scrolls would be exactly the same. There is a very beautiful hadith in the Musnad of Imam Ahmed, volume number 43 and hadith number 26031.

It is a Hadith from our mother Aisha RA. Prophet SAW said, "There are three separate types of registrars. There is a registrar that Allah SWT will not care about it. There is a registrar, nothing that is in it will be neglected. Then there is a registrar that Allah SWT will not forgive it. As for the register that Allah SWT will never forgive, it is the Registrar of shirk".

If a person dies having committed shirk and having not repented from it, then the Prophet SAW says that, "Who ever does Shirk, Allah SWT has made Jannah haram for him". So, we firmly believe that the only unforgivable sin that is in Islam is the sin of shirk when it is done without repentance.

As for the first registrar that Allah SWT will not care about, this is the personal sins that a person does between him and Allah SWT. Maybe he didn't fast properly. That he left a salah that he shouldn't have left. So, these personal sins, Allah SWT shall forgive and overlook to whomever he wants.

Now, this 'whomever he wants' is the key phrase here. Because what it implies is that, for those whom Allah SWT 'does not want', these sins shall be accounted for. And this is why we get to the issue of the reality of sins. Those whose sins are minor; their good deeds shall observe all of the minor sins. So, for this register, Allah SWT will not even care about, if you have only done minor sins and you avoided the major sins.

You will not go to Jahannam for minor sins. You might get punished in other ways. As for major sins, it is up to Allah SWT. If he wants, he shall forgive, or not forgive.

As for the third registrar that Allah SWT will not leave anything from that register. This is the Zulm that people do to one another. This is you back biting, or slandering, or stealing, or stabbing, or causing any harm or injustice to somebody else. Our Prophet SAW said, "You're going to have to deal with one another. There is no divine intervention between two people doing Zulm to one another".

So, we need to be aware that there's going to be basically three types of registrars. We need to make sure we have nothing in the shirk category. Then we need to make sure we have nothing in the harm to others category. We don't want to come with another person accusing of doing injustice or harm against him. That is the one Allah SWT will not intervene.

Even if Allah SWT wants to forgive the sins between you and him, in Allah SWT's infinite justice, when you have harmed another person, then Allah SWT will allow those two people to deal amongst themselves. And on that day, the currency will not be gold or silver. The currency will not be dollars or pounds. The currency will not be Bitcoin and paper currency. The currency will be the currency of good deeds and evil deeds.

Therefore, beware of going around hurting other people, harming other people, slandering other people, stealing the money of other people. Beware you who backbites and gossips. Beware you who discusses the honor of chaste men and women. Beware those who are causing Zulm and fitna and facade amongst other people. That even if your good deeds are as high as the skies, on the day of judgment, Allah SWT will allow every single person whose honor you tarnished, who's Zulm that you were guilty of, to get their share.

On that day every single Mazloum will be able to get the Haq directly from the one who did Zulm to him. And Allah SWT being the perfect King, will not intervene. The one who has done Zulm shall face the consequences of his Zulm. On that day those who are Mazloum will be greedy for every good deed.

So those who have done Zulm repent to Allah SWT in this world before repentance is of no use. Prophet SAW said, "O Muslim, beware of causing any Zulm in this world to any other human being. As for the sins between you and Allah SWT, ask Allah SWT's forgiveness and hope for the best."

Good Deeds for Scrolls

Now in a number of narrations, our Prophet SAW recommended that we do certain things so that we find them in our Scrolls. This shows us that there are things that we should be doing with the intent of making sure that we find them in the Scrolls on the day of judgement.

Of them is the Hadith of Prophet SAW reported in Ibn Majah, that the Prophet SAW said, "How fortunate is the one who finds in his Scrolls a lot of Istighfar". Here the Prophet SAW is asking us to remember that we're going to meet all of our deeds with the Scrolls in the day of judgment. So, he's reminding us that it will be good news for us if we find a lot of Istighfar in our Scrolls the day of judgment. For this we should do a lot of Istighfar in our worldly life.

In the Hadith narrated in Musnad Imam Ahmed, Umar RA passed by Talha Ibn Zubair RA, and he found him to be very worried, very grieved. Umar RA said, "What is the matter with you? Has something irritated you? What is going on? Why are you so grieved?"

Talha RA said that, "I heard the Prophet SAW say that there is 1 Kalema, one phrase that if a person were to say it when he was to die, he would find his Scroll full of light. But I don't know that Kalema. What is that Kalema that our Prophet SAW mentioned?"

Umar RA said, "I will tell you. This it is the same Kalema that out Prophet SAW wanted his uncle to say, Shahadat La Ilaha Il Allah". When Umar RA told him this, all of the grief left Talha RA, and he became very happy that he heard this knowledge from Umar RA.

So, whoever says the Kalema at the time of death, his Scroll of good deeds will be good deeds of light. I ask Allah SWT that our last Kalema in this world ever be "La Ilaha Ill Allah" and you as well make that Dua. Because we want to have that Kalema.

We also know that the Kalema of "La Ilaha Ill Allah" will be even on the separate scroll. It is going to be so powerful and so weighty. We know this from the Hadith that, on the day of judgement a man will come and he will have 99 Scrolls of evil deeds, as far as the eye can see. Those Scrolls will be put on one side of the scale.

Then Allah SWT will say, "Do you have any good deeds?" The man will think and he will not be able to think of any good deed. Then a small parchment is going to be brought out and Allah SWT will say, "Actually you do have a good deed". And on this card will be the Kalema of "La Ilaha Ill Allah". The man will say, "O Allah SWT, of what use is this card against the 99 Scrolls on the other side?"

Allah SWT will say, "On this day No Zulm will be shown and even the smallest and the greatest of deeds will be made Hisab of". Then of course, his Iman will be heavier than all of the evil deeds, and he shall be forgiven. Our Scholars mention that this is an exceptional scenario. Generally speaking, good deeds also have to be on your scrolls as well.

This also shows us that the Scrolls would be of different sizes, depending on the quantity and the quality of a deed.

Hisab

Now we move on to the next issue and that is the issue of counting of deeds. We have reference this a few times about this issue of all of these different aspects happening one after the other. Actually, the Hisab or counting of deeds and the Scrolls go hand-in-hand.

But there are many hadiths about the Hisab and there are many Hadiths about the Scrolls. Therefore, we are doing them step by step. Even though chronologically, it does appear that the Hisab and the scrolls are going to happen hand-in-hand.

Now Hisab in Arabic means to count. That's why mathematics is called the Ilm Al Hisab. So, it's an issue of calculating. The accountant is called Muhasib. The issue of Hisab means that you're going to essentially account for or count each and everything.

The concept of Hisab is self-evident. Which is that every single deed of mankind, good or bad, is going to be accounted for, line by line, bit by bit. There are categories of people who will have a difficult Hisab. There are categories of people who will have an easy Hisab.

There are literally dozens of verses about the concept of Hisab. We cannot go over all of them. There are that many in quantity. We'll just mention some of them. For example, in Surah Ghafir verse 17 Allah SWT mentions, "Today everybody will get what they did. No Injustice will be done today, and Allah SWT is quick in reckoning".

So, Allah SWT will reckon every single person for all they have done, and Allah SWT will do it in the twinkling of an eye. Also, the Quran tells us that the people who rejected Allah SWT, "They weren't expecting that the Hisab will take place. They didn't want that to happen".

And we learned that Allah SWT will directly take charge of the Hisab. That no Angel, no intermediary, but Allah SWT himself will do the Hisab of each and every person. Imagine this dear Muslims, every single one of us will have to stand in front of Allah SWT individually. Allah SWT will speak to us and make Hisab of our lives and our deeds line by line. There will be no one between us and Allah SWT.

Even our Prophet SAW is reminded in the Quran that, "You are not the one who's going to make their Hisab". In fact, he is told in the Quran in multiple versus, "Your Job is to convey, and it is our job to do with the Hisab".

There are many Hadiths as well that mention the concept of Hisab and the fact that we have to face the Hisab on the day of Judgment. Of them is the famous Hadith in the Musnad of Imam Ahmed, that our Prophet SAW said, "Two are the things that the son of Adam does not like, and those two things are death and to not have a lot of money".

Then the Prophet SAW mentions two points that are positive about these two things. He said, "Dying is better for the believer then being subjugated to tests and trials". Subhan Allah, how true this is. Those that are suffering from calamities, from civil wars, those suffering from issues, even the irritation of Covid-19 that we are all suffering from; there are those that lived good lives, long life and they moved on. They didn't have to see this. There is some mercy in it for them.

So, to not be tested and pass, is better than to be tested and fail. So, to not be tested is a blessing. So, our Prophet SAW is saying, to die is better than to be tested.

Then he SAW Said, "And the son of Adam also does not like that he is poor. But being poor means, you have a smaller Hisab". So, the rich will have a longer Hisab. The rich will have much more auditing to do for every single penny that they earned and they spent. But the poor will have a quicker Hisab.

There is a weak Narration that the poor people will enter Jannah 500 years before the rich people, as they will clear their Hisab earlier. But the concept does seem to have an element of authenticity to it, because the rich people have to account for more.

Now Hisab will be done for every single person, in every single Ummah. We know this from many Hadiths. Of them is the Hadith in Sahih Muslim that our Prophet SAW said, "There was a man of the nation's before you, that his Hisab was made of on the day of judgement. And they didn't find anything good in his Hisab, except that he was a man who would give out loans to people and he would tell his servants that if they found somebody who couldn't pay back the loan, don't be harsh or strict with them in this regard, and be gentle".

So, when the Hisab was being done, Allah SWT will say, "I have more rights to exude this generosity and gentleness then this person. Therefore, I am asking that his sins be overlooked".

Here we find that this person, he didn't have a lot of Salah, he didn't have a lot of Zakat, he didn't have a lot of good deeds that other people link to piety. But He had a kind heart and soul. He was a rich person and he would give money, but he needed it back. He was not giving charity.

But he would tell his servants that if somebody is in a difficult circumstance, don't be harsh and be gentle. Collect money later. He did it from a pure heart. Subhan Allah, something as small as this can help someone in Akhirah. Because Allah SWT is Ar-Rehman and Ar-Rahim.

However, of the blessings of our Prophet SAW is that our Ummah will be the first, upon which Hisab is done. That's a blessing because we don't want to wait. Our Prophet SAW said, "We are the last and yet we are the first". Meaning, we are the last of the Ummahs. Chronologically there is no Ummah after the Ummah of the Prophet SAW. And We are the first on whom Hisab will be made. Because on the day of judgment, an announcement will be made, "Where is the unlettered Ummah and its Prophet?" Then we will be brought in front of all other nations.

Chronologically of Hisab

Now, chronologically when will the Hisab take place? Some Ulema, including Al Qurtubi RA, say that the Hisab will take place after the Scrolls are handed to the people. Their interpretation of the text is that first and foremost there's going to be Allah SWT looking up on the creation. Then the scrolls will be handed to people. Then after this will be the Hisab.

The scroll will be handed in the right hand or in the left hand. Then after that, there is going to be a line by line Hisab. They base it on the verse in the Quran, "The one who's given the book in his right hand he shall be given an easy Hisab". So, it seems that the Hisab will take place after the books are handed over.

They also base it on the verse in the Quran, "The one who is given his book in his left hand will say, 'Woe to me. I wish I was not given this book and I don't know what my Hisab is going to be". Based on this, the scholars say that this clearly demonstrates that the Hisab will take place after the scrolls are handed. There is definitely a strong case to be made.

Other group of Scholar say that the verse is not implying chronology. In fact, the concept of the Scrolls and the concept of the Hisab are simultaneous. They are not one after the other. Rather the interpretation of the verses is that Allah SWT is saying that, "Those who get their

Scrolls in the right hands, they would have had easy reckoning".

Now, there is an explicit Hadith that does seem to very clearly indicate that the Hisab and the Scrolls are in fact simultaneous. They're taking place at the same time. That the scrolls are going to be handed and the Hisab is being done right there and then you are told the results right there. In the end, Allah knows best.

Categories of Hisab

Now in terms of the categories of Hisab, and the types of people that will or will not face Hisab; Al Qurtubi RA mentions that there are three categories of people. Number one, those who will not have any Hisab at all. They will simply be handed the Scrolls and they will have zero Hisab.

This is the highest category. It is mentioned in the number of Hadith that they will enter Jannah without Hisab. Number two, the majority of the believers will have an easy Hisab. Number 3, there's going to be a difficult Hisab. According to Al Qurtubi RA, these are the disbelievers and the weak Muslims.

The point is that there are 3 categories. That much is definitely explicit in the Quran and the Sunnah. First is evident in Sunnah, but not the Quran, that there will be people who will enter Jannah without Hisab. Second are those that will have an easy Hisab. Third are those that will have a difficult Hisab. This is very much confirmed.

Also there does appear to be a fourth category of Hisab for a very select group of people, and that is the Prophets AS. The Prophet AS have to account for things that are very different than what we have to account for. They have to account for what their Ummahs have done to them.

This is quite explicit in the Quran, Surah A'raf verse 6, "We are going to ask those whom the Prophets AS came to and we're going to ask the Prophets AS". So, asking the Prophets AS is separate. Also, in Surah Maida verse 109, "The day that Allah SWT will gather all the Prophets AS and Allah SWT will ask them, 'What response did you get?'".

This is a very special category of people. Those are the Prophets AS. They have a different set of questions than the rest of us and that is fully understandable.

We also learn from the Hadith of the Prophet SAW narrated by Aisha RA, that the Prophet SAW would make dua to Allah SWT that, "O Allah SWT give me an easy Hisab". So, Aisha RA said, "Ya Rasool Allah SAW, what is this easy Hisab?"

The Prophet SAW said, "Whoever is going have to go over point by point, whoever is going to be put on the interrogation, that this is going to be a type of punishment". Aisha RA says, "Doesn't Allah SWT say in the Quran that Hisab will be a blessing for the believers? Then how will it be a punishment?"

The Prophet SAW said, "That this blessing that you mentioned is the general examination. But whoever is going to be forced to defend each and every point, that in and of itself is a type of punishment". In another version of the Hadith, the Prophet SAW said, "The blessing will be an easy Hisab, where his book will be looked at, and then will be overlooked. However, whoever has to go over line-by-line that will be the person who will be destroyed".

Now what this means is that for example, in some countries the government audits your taxes. So, the year that it doesn't audit the taxes, it just overlooks them. This is equivalent of an easy Hisab. But the year that they audit you and they ask you to provide proofs of every line and number in your tax return, that entire process in and of itself is the type of punishment.

Now, imagine if we are worried about the annual tax return for our governments, how about our entire life's deeds that we have to account for in front of Allah SWT? We don't want that. We ask Allah SWT for an easy Hisab.

We also learn that there's going to be an elite group of people who's Hisab will be completely overlooked and that's something that is a beautiful goal that we should all strive for.

In a Hadith narrated by Ibn Abbas RA, The Prophet SAW said, "I saw all of the Ummahs on the day of judgement. There I saw a Prophet AS, that had a small group with him. I saw other Prophets AS, who had only one or even two people with them. I even saw a Prophet AS, who didn't have a single follower at all. Then a large gathering was shown to me, and I thought that is my Ummah. But it was said to me that it is Musa AS and his people. Then I was asked to look at the horizon, and I saw another great gathering. Then I was told that, that was my Ummah. And that, from them, 70000 will enter Jannah without any Hisab and without any Azab".

Then the famous Sahabi Ukasha RA stood up and he said, "Ya Rasool Allah SAW, ask Allah SWT that he puts me amongst those 70000". The Prophet SAW said, "You are going to be from them". Then another person stood up and he asked the same thing. The Prophet SAW said, "Ukasha RA preceded you."

Now, it's not just 70000 that will Jannah without any Hisab. We learn that there's going to be more than 70000. In one narration it says for every thousand, another 70000 will be allowed. Another narration says that, Allah SWT fills up his palms and gave them to the Prophet SAW, and said, "All of these as well will enter Jannah without Hisab".

These are going to be the greatest of the believers to enter Jannah without Hisab. That is what we want. We don't even want to even have an easy Hisab.

Private Hisab

Also, of the beautiful things that we learn is that, the Hisab for the believers will be private. It will not be public. As for those who rejected Allah SWT, and for those who have done Zulm, their Hisab will be public and it will be humiliating.

We seek Allah SWT's refuge. But imagine being brought on the day of judgment and everybody can hear your sins and your personal crimes. Everybody knows what this person has done. What a great embarrassment and humiliation it is. That is why we ask Allah SWT to protect us from the humiliation of this world and of the next World.

That's why the humiliation of the next world is the worst humiliation. As the Quran mentions, because to be humiliated on the day of judgment means that Allah SWT has removed all mercy from you. We seek protection from that. Because to be protected and to have no humiliation is a great blessing from Allah SWT.

There's a beautiful Hadith in Sahih Muslim, which is really a very touching and a very emotional Hadith. It is from Ibn Umar RA. That he was doing Tawaf around the Ka'bah, and somebody came up to him and held on to his hand.

Then that man said, "Tell me the Hadith that you heard from the Prophet SAW about the Najwa". The Najwa is the private booth or the private a covering that Allah SWT will do the Hisab for the believers in. The Hisab will be done between Allah SWT and the servant, and it will be shielded from the eyes of all other people. The word Najwa in Arabic means 'in secrecy' or 'in private'.

Allah SWT says in the Quran that, "Secret Gatherings are not good unless it is meant for something that is good". There is something called Najwa on the day of judgment and that is going to be a secret between Allah SWT and between the servant.

The man had heard that Ibn Umar RA had been narrating this hadith. So, he went up him and asked about it. Ibn Umar RA said, "I heard the Prophet SAW say that Allah SWT will come close to the believer and Allah SWT will envelope him with his covering. Allah SWT will then ask him about his sins. The believer will agree to his sins. He will go on admitting to every single thing that he has done. Then in his heart, he will think that he is destroyed".

Then Allah SWT will ask him, if he has any excuse for his sins. The man will say, "No, my Lord, I don't have any excuse". Allah SWT will say, "Did my Witnesses of the Angels write everything correctly or do you doubt it that they are lying?" He will say, "No my Lord. They are not lying. The wrote everything correctly". Then the man will think that he is gone, because all of these things have been mentioned. Then Allah SWT will say, "I covered these sins from the eyes of others in this world, and I will forgive them for you on this day".

So, we ask Allah SWT for his covering and for his forgiveness. The Hadith then says that, he will be given his book, and he will take it from the right hand. This is a beautiful Hadith for many reasons.

Of them is that it demonstrates that even the believer will have some type of Hisab. This shows us that there are many levels of Hisab. This is not an example of an Easy Hisab. This one is a lower level or a difficult Hisab. Easy Hisab is where everything is overlooked and the person is simply asked to enter Jannah.

This person is a sinner, who was also a repented person. This person is a righteous sinner. So, yes you can be righteous in some aspects and be a sinner in another aspect. There are people that are sinners and they have good deeds as well.

For these categories of people, Allah SWT will go over there Hisab line by line. But because they had good deeds as well, and because they had piety, and Iman; therefore, on the day of judgment they shall be covered up by the covering of Allah SWT, and they will not be humiliated in front of all the people.

Then Allah will say, "I covered up your sins in this world. Your sins, you know them and I knew them. But mankind did not know them. And they did not know them, because I from my Rehma covered those sins. I from my mercy concealed those sins from the eyes of others. Even your close family and your friends, even your spouse and your parents, did not know these sins. Because I covered them up for you in the dunya. Just like I did it in the dunya, now I will continue that covering and I will cover them up in this world as well".

Then he will be given the Hisab and he scrolls. This clearly shows us, and this Hadid it is explicit, that the scrolls are given after the Hisab. Within the same time frame. The concept of the Scrolls being given and Hisab taking place is not one after the other. It is simultaneous. That is very explicit from this Hadith. The Hisab is being done as the scrolls are being unrolled and then given back to you.

Then the Prophet SAW said, "As for the Kafir and as for the Munafiq, then in front of all of mankind, it will be announced. These are the people that lied against Allah SWT. Allah SWT curses upon the Zalimeen".

Ibn Kathir RA in his Treatise on the day of judgement, mentions narration that goes back to Abu Huraira RA. It is a similar narration to that from Ibn Umar RA. It also says that, "Allah SWT will come closer to his servant on the day of judgement, and Allah SWT will conceal and cover his servant, and Allah SWT will then give the book to his servant, and he will say, 'Read the book'. Every single time the servant finds a good deed, his face will brighten up, and he will thank Allah SWT. He will fall down in Sajda. Every time he comes across a bad deed, he will feel guilty and bad and his heart will tremble and his face will darken with fear. Allah SWT will say to him, 'Do you have any excuse?' He will say, 'No'. Then Allah SWT will say, 'Know that I have forgiven it for you'."

The people on the outside of this this concealment will only see him fall down and they will not hear the negative things until finally it will be announced that this person is going to Jannah.

Punishment with In Hisab

The concept is that once again there is a detailed Hisab taking place and there is a slight element of punishment here. This shows us that, whoever has to go over line-by-line is being punished. But it does not mean that whoever is going line by line, will go to Jahannam.

Rather there are people who have done sins but they don't deserve to go to Jahannam. Allah SWT will forgive them for their good deeds. So, they will undergo certain trials, that are painful, and that are torturous in their own way. But the purpose for that is, so that the sins they have done are expunged because of those trials.

Now, one of the trials, which is a very difficult one, is to answer to Allah SWT directly for every single crime and to have to explain to Allah SWT why you did it. Even though in the end Allah SWT knows you will be forgiven because of other good deeds. But we don't know what's going to happen.

Because there are going to be people, they have to go through all of the Hisab and then they will go to Jahannam after that. That is why we do not want to be in that category.

We either want to have an easy Hisab in which case we are just handed the book and there's no detailed or line by line Hisab. Or even better than this, and that is without any Hisab. That's our goal. You do not want to be in this category of line by line.

But our Prophet SAW is telling us that even in that category, there is hope that not everybody who gets in this category is automatically going to Jahannam. There will be people, they have evil deeds that have to be accounted for. But they also have good deed. So, Allah SWT will go over line-by-line, and in that will be their punishment.

Then by the time they're done, their punishment is over, and Allah SWT will say, 'You're forgiven. Go to Jannah'. Alhamdulillah, that is great. But we'd rather not go through that and enter Jannah directly.

Hisab of Blood and Salah

Now, what are two of the most important things that will be asked about on the day of judgement? In A hadith in Sahih Bukhari, our Prophet SAW said that, "The first matter that will be dealt with between the people, the first issue in the Hisab will be with regards to blood".

The meaning of blood here is if a person murdered another person. So, murderers are the first category of people that will have to answer to Allah SWT. Now, if this is the case of somebody who has committed 1 murder, what do you think will happen to those tyrants, those dictators and those kings, who think that they are so mighty, that they are destroying hundreds of thousands, even millions of their own, or other people?

What do you think of the empires that are destroying innocent people? Will not there Azab come back on them in the Akhira? if one murderer will be brought forth in front of Allah SWT, and that is going to be the first Hisab; what do you think of the one who has killed a million or more than this?

What would you think of the one who has tortured innocent scholars and has thrown them into jail? one who has killed an innocent Muslim for no reason other than that he wants to defend his honor, his land, or his properties?

What do you think of the evil tyrants who want to take their land and homes from these people? They will have to answer to Allah SWT. Indeed, Allah SWT will do a just Hisab, and we leave their affair to Allah SWT. These people need to repent to Allah SWT before it is too late.

This applies to all of us, if we have any Zulm that we have done to other people, and especially the wort Zulm, which is the shedding the lives of innocent people. We have to remember, the first matter to be dealt with on the day of judgment would be about blood shed between people.

In another version of the Hadith, the Prophet SAW said, "The first matter that a person will be asked about, on the day of judgment on the Hisab is his Salah. If his Salah is in order, the rest of the Hisab will be easy, and he should be saved. If the Salah is not in order, then the rest will be destroyed and lost".

Now, the first hadith where the Prophet SAW is saying that the first question of Hisab is about blood, is when the Hisab is between two people. The other Hadith that is talking about Salah, that Hisab is between Allah and Mankind.

Also, in the second Hadith, we learn that one of the strongest mechanisms to guarantee that we have an easy Hisab is to concentrate on Salah. As the Prophet SAW said, if the first matter of Salah is in order, then the rest of Hisab will be in order. Meaning Allah SWT will overlook res of it. But if the Salah is not in order, then the rest of the Hisab will be difficult.

So, if we protect the Salah, if we guarantee we have the five Salah done properly, if we are regular in our Salah, then Insha'Allah, we will be from those who are in the easy Hisab category. As long as we have not done Zulm to other people. Because that's a separate category all together. If it's just between us and Allah SWT, we can be hopeful of being saved from punishment.

Hisab of Deeds and Blessings

For other questions that we are going to be asked about in the Hisab, Allah SWT says in Surah Al-Hijr that, "We will ask every one of them about what deeds they used to do".

So, a part of the Hisab is that we're going to be asked about is our deeds. We're going to be asked about our actions. Also, we are going to be asked about our blessings. Allah SWT will ask us about our blessings. Now, realize this happen to people in the third category. Those who are going to go line by line. They will be asked about every deed. They will be asked about every single blessing as well.

There is a beautiful Hadith in Sahih Muslim, that one day the Prophet SAW, Abu Bakr RA, and Umar RA were all hungry because they had nothing to eat. They were all sitting outside at the time of lunch. Until finally one of the Sahaba saw this, and he could not bear this. He invited them to his house. He slaughtered an animal. Then he fed them the animal, and they then eat from this animal, and then thanked Allah SWT.

Then our Prophet SAW said, "I swear by the one in whose hands is my life, that you will be asked about this blessing on the day of judgment. You left your house hungry and then you only came back after your stomachs were full with this blessing".

Therefore, this concept of being asked about our blessings is something that is very clear. That we will be asked Allah SWT gave you this blessing, what did you do with it.

In Quran as well, in Surah Takathur, "Then you will be asked about your blessings". In Surah Al Isra verse 36, "Verily your hearing and you're seeing, and your chest, your intelligence and your awareness, all of this you will be asked about". Meaning Allah SWT will ask you; "Did I not give you faculties of intellect, of hearing, of seeing?"

In another Hadith, our Prophet SAW said, "The two feet of the son of Adam will not move on the day of judgment until he is asked the five questions. Number one, about his life and what did he do with his life. Number two, about his knowledge and how much he acted upon that knowledge. Number 3, about his money and where did the earn it from. Number four, where did he spend it on. Number 5, his health and his body, what did he do with his health and his body that we gave him".

Can you imagine, if you enter the classroom, and at the beginning of the semester, the first thing that the professor did is that he handed out the final exam. He said, 'These are the questions. If you know your questions, you're going to pass'. Can you imagine any student who is going to fail the exam? So, Allah SWT has handed us the questions.

In the Hadith of Tirmidhi as well, our Prophet SAW said that, "The first blessing that Allah SWT will ask a person about will be his health. And Allah SWT will say, "Didn't we give you a healthy body? And didn't we give you cold water to drink? We gave you all that you needed. What did you do with your life on this earth?'" This is a very explicit narration that Allah SWT is going to ask us for every single blessing.

There is another Hadith in Muslim that the Prophet SAW said that, "Allah SWT will meet a person on the day of Judgment, And Allah SWT will ask him, "Wasn't I generous to you? And didn't I give you wealth? Didn't I give you money? Didn't I give you children? Didn't I give you horses? And I left you to grow healthy. I left you two enjoy all of this".

The man will say, "Yes you did O Allah SWT". Then Allah SWT will say, "Did you ever think that you would meet me?" The man will say, "No". So, Allah SWT will say, "Just like you neglected me, I too will neglect you now".

This is a very clear Hadith that the person who didn't care about Allah SWT or the next life, the person who even if he lived a good life in this world, even if you try to do some good deeds in this world, but he didn't think about a higher cause, he didn't think about here after; that this person is in a state of heedlessness. So, Allah SWT will neglect them on the day of judgment.

Then another person will come, and the same questions will be given, and the man will say there, "Oh my Lord, I believed in you, and I worshipped you, and I believed in your Prophet, and I prayed, and I fasted, and I gave charity, and I did as much good as I could".

The other person will then be testifying on his behalf, the good deeds are going to come, and he shall enter Jannah. The point being that both of these people will be asked by Allah SWT about his blessings. This is all the parts of the Hisab.

Frist People Hisab Will be Made Against

Also, some categories of people will be given to Hisab before other categories of people. Not all the Hisab will take place at the same time. Some categories of people will be judged before other categories. The most famous Hadith in this regard is the Hadith in Sahih Muslim, which is really a Hadith that should terrify all of us. This Hadith it implies that those who do things insincerely will be punished before others.

It is the famous Hadith of Abu Huraira RA. Our Prophet SAW asked Abu Huraira RA, "Do you know the first three people whose Hisab will be done on the day of judgement?" Abu Huraira RA said, "I don't know. Allah SWT and his Messenger SAW know best". The Prophet SAW said that, "In the first person, a mujahid, the warrior will come. The mujahid who is slain and martyred in the way of Allah SWT".

Allah SWT will say to him that, "Didn't I give you everything?" Then he will say, "Yes". Allah SWT will say, "What did you do with that?" The man will stand up with pride and say, "O Allah SWT, I fought and I fought, with courage and bravery, and I fought until I was killed in your way as a shaheed". Allah SWT will say, "You lie. You did not fight for me. You fought for your own ego. You fought so that people could praise you as courageous and as warrior. So, your reward will be with them".

Then the reciter of the Quran will be brought, or the scholar will be brought. Allah SWT will say, "Didn't I give everything?" He will say, "Yes". Then Allah SWT will say, "What did you do with that?" They will say that, "We recited the Quran and we taught it". Then Allah SWT will say, "You lie. You did not teach the Quran to the people for my sake. You taught so that the people can call you a scholar. That is what they said. So, get your reward from them".

Then the third person will be a person who was generous with his money. He was always feeding the poor and helping the sick. Allah SWT will ask him, "Did I not give you everything?" He will say, "Yes". Allah SWT will say, "What did you do that?" Man will say, "O Allah SWT, I was generous my whole life. I gave and I gave". Allah SWT will say, "You were not generous for my sake. You were generous so that your reputation could be established. So that people could call you generous. So, go get your reward from them".

Then the Prophet SAW tapped Abu Huraira RA on the knee and he said, "O Abu Huraira RA, these are the first three people that Hisab will be made against on the day of judgement". So, Hisab will be done in different categories. For some people of the Ummah of the Prophet SAW, an early Hisab is a blessing. For other people, an early Hisab Is a punishment. It all depends on what is going on in that case.

Testimonies and Evidence

Now, we move on to the issue of the testimonies of the Hisab and the issue of evidence. There will be testimonies and there will be witnesses on the day of judgment. Just like in any court case, in any trial, there will be testimony. Same way there are going to be exhibits and they're going to be Witnesses in each person's trial.

These will be the actual deeds or the effects of the deeds. They will be brought forth and witnesses will be your own body. Allah SWT says that, "On that day, we're going to see all their mouths. And their hands and their feet are going to testify against them".

Allah SWT says in Surah Fussilat that, "Their skins testified against them. And when they're able to speak, they're going to say, 'Why did you testify against us?" And the skins will reply back that, 'The one who caused you to speak, also caused us to speak as well'."

The Hadith in Sahih Muslim states that the man will say that, "O Allah SWT, I don't accept the testimony of this Angel. I don't accept and reject the book". So, Allah SWT will say, "Are you fine if I bring a witness?" The man will say, "Yes. As long as I agree to the witness". Allah SWT will say, "Fine". The man in his heart will think, "I'm not going to accept any witness".

Then Allah SWT is going to make him a witness against his own self. How can you then refute, when his tongue, his body, his hands, and his legs will speak. So, this is very clear that testimonies are going to happen.

Also, the Quran will be an exhibit. So, Quran will be testifying for or against every single person. According to some interpretations, the earth and the land will itself testify. The Quran says that, "On that day, the earth is going to be shaking and it is going to mention its news".

That is this news? "Whoever does an Atom's weight of good and whoever does an atoms weight of evil on the surface of the earth will be brought forth".

Also, we learn in the Hadith that, everything that hears the Azan of the Moazin will testify for him. Also, the one who says 'Labaik Allah Huma Labaik", every rock and every tree that heard it will testify for him. So, we learn from this that in this Hisab there will be exhibits and there will be witnesses.

As for the exhibits, they will be either the Quran itself, or things that have seen us doo certain deeds. Ask for the witnesses, some people's own bodies will testify against them. All of this will be taking place before scrolls are going to be handed over.

Reckoning for Zulm and Injustices

Now, the next point of discussion will be the issue of the creation suing one another in the court of Allah SWT. This is called Iqtisas. This means that each person is going to get the right due from other people, that took their rights in this world.

When we mentioned the issue of the Scrolls, the issue of Hisab, the issue of Allah SWT reckoning us; However, there will be a special type of reckoning for the Zulm and the injustices that are taking place in between the creation.

So, if you slander somebody, hurt somebody, stole money from somebody, punch somebody, kill somebody; if you did something to hurt another person, that person has the right to sue you on the day of judgment in the court of Allah SWT.

Irrespective of the Final Destination

There is a famous Hadith of Sahih Bukhari, and there are many wordings of it in many books of Hadiths. It is a famous Hadith of Abdullah ibn Unais RA, who said, he heard the Prophet SAW say that, "On the day of judgment people will be resurrected naked and uncircumcised, and without any belongings. They are not going to have nothing with them. Then Allah SWT will shout out to them with a voice, that those who are close by will be able to hear that voice the same way, that those who are far. And those who are far will be able to hear it the same way as those were close".

Then Allah SWT will say, "I am the king. I am the judge. It is not permitted for anybody who is from the people of the fire of hell, that before he enters the fire of hell, if anyone has anything that is due to him from the people of Jannah, that reckoning must be done. And it is not befitting that there's a single person that is going to Jannah and the person of Jahannam has a Haq that is due to him, except that he will get that Haq. Even it is a slap, or even a punch, or a hit, that was done in that world, they have this right".

One of the Sahaba said, "O Messenger of Allah SWT, you just said that we would come naked, and barefoot, and uncircumcised, and without having any of our belongings. So how is there going to be any judgment? With what are we going to be handing things back and forth?"

The Prophet SAW said, "With the good and the bad deeds". That is how they just this is going to be meted out.

Now this Hadith is very profound for one simple reason. It doesn't matter if you're going to Jannah or Jahannam. It doesn't matter if you're a person of Jannah and you wrong somebody who's going to Jahannam. Although, he's going to Jahannam, no one will enter Jannah, except that his complaint against the person of Jannah is resolved.

So, piety will not get away from you the crime of doing an injustice to somebody else. You doing an injustice makes you an impious person. Even if the one that you do an injustice to is somebody was rejected Allah SWT. Or is somebody who might be doing other Injustices in his or her own life. But if you are doing your own injustice to this person, then you need to resolve that right then and there. This shows us the infinite justice of Allah SWT and the perfection of Allah SWT.

Make it Halal

In the famous Hadith of Sahih Bukhari, our Prophet SAW said that, "whoever has done any Zulm to his brother, whoever has done any injustice to his brother, whether it is to do with his honor, or anything other than that, then let him make this Zulm Halal. Untie it and get rid of it, before the day in which there will be no gold and silver. Rather it will be the deeds that will be taken in response for the amount of Zulm, that he will have done. And if he does not have good deed, then the bad deeds of the other person will be taken and then given to him".

This Hadith also shows us that we are being commanded by our Prophet SAW to make sure that if you've done anything wrong in this Dunya, then make sure that you get rid of it in this Dunya. Now, notice he began with the issue of honor. If you have harmed the honor of another person. How do you harm the honor of somebody?

You harm the honor of somebody with your tongue, with your Ghibat, with your backbiting, with your slander. So, if you have said something that is not true, or even if it is true, but it is backbiting; if you have done something that will hurt the dignity and the honor of your brother, our Prophet SAW has asked us to make sure that you resolve it in this Dunya, before the day of judgment.

Because that day there will be no golden silver, rather in that day it will be good deeds and bad deeds. Can you imagine, you have done your salah, you have done your Zakat, you have done your fasting in Ramadan, all of that hard-earned deeds, going to someone else?

Can you imagine if somebody just took your money from you? That a large amount to fine came in and 50% of your wealth went away. Wouldn't you feel grieved? Imagine your good deeds being given to other people, simply because you did not act wisely and you hurt other people. That you said things, you did things, you stole thing.

The Bankrupt Person

In a hadith in Sahih Muslim, and in other books, our Prophet SAW asked the Sahaba, he said, "Do you know who is the bankrupt person?" They said, "O Messenger of Allah SAW the bankrupt person amongst us is the one who's debts are more than what he owns. He doesn't have anything".

Our Prophet SAW said, "No. The real bankrupt person from my Ummah is the one that will come on the day of judgment with lots of Salah and Zakat and Fast. He will come with good deeds like mountains. But at the same time, he has cursed one person, and he has slandered another person, and he has eaten the wealth of a third person, and he has shed the blood of another person".

The Prophet SAW said, "Every one of them will be given from his good deed. Until if all of his good deeds are finished and he still owes things, then the sins of the ones he wronged will then be put on him, and it will be burdened with him. Then he shall be cast into the fire of hell".

This is a terrifying Hadith. Because it shows us that you can come with the right amount of Salah and Zakat, and Fast. You can come with the rituals been performed. You can come looking pious. But you have harmed too many people. That you have done too many backstabbing, and your tongue has been used to hurt and irritate lots of people. So, all the good deeds will be of no use on the day of judgement.

This really shows us the mistakes of those people in our community that emphasize the rituals so much and they forget the issue of Akhlaq and manners. Our religion is the religion of the middle. Neither do we say that the rituals are more important. Nor do we say that the Akhlaq are more important. We say that the righteous Muslim has both rituals and Akhlaq together.

We need both of them. If you only have one and not the other, it will be highly problematic on the day of judgment. Because you have not fulfilled the criteria of what it means to be a good Muslim.

Rights of Weak and Oppressed

There's a beautiful Hadith reported in Sunnah ibn Majah, that once our Prophet SAW was sitting with the Muhajiroun that had Just come back from Abyssinia. He said to them that, "Can you tell me something interesting or amazing that you saw in the land of Abyssinia?" One of them said, "Yes, O Messenger Allah SWT". It's a really interesting story.

He said, "Once when we were sitting in Abyssinia, and an old lady came. She was one of the wives of their priests. She was carrying a jug of water on her on head. When she was walking by, there was a group of ruffians there. One of them stood up and he pushed her so hard from behind, that she fell down on to her knees. The Jug on her head fell and it splattered and it cracked everywhere. Then they were laughing".

The lady turned around and she said that, "O you treacherous fool, O you evil person, what will be your state, the day that Allah SWT brings his Throne, and gathers together all of mankind, and the limbs will be speaking out. On that day, you shall see what will be the verdict between us, and what is going to happen on that day".

Our Prophet SAW said, "She has spoken the truth. Indeed, she has spoken the truth. How can Allah SWT ever bless a nation that does not guarantee the rights of the poor against the rights of the powerful".

The main point here is that the Prophet SAW affirmed that she is speaking the truth. When she said that those people who teased her, those people who were rough to her, pushed her and the water jug fell and broke; and she's irritated and embarrassed and hurt; she said, "There is the day of judgment between us and we shall resolve our dispute on the day of judgment". The Prophet SAW said, "She is speaking the truth".

This really shows us how important it is to give the rights of those who are weak, and those were oppressed. So that we do not oppress them. And we make sure that the rich and the powerful do not get away with oppression, because they are rich and powerful.

Responding to Evil with Evil

Now, what if somebody did something bad to you, and in return, you did something bad to them? Allah SWT says in the Quran, "The response of one evil is to return it to the same amount of evil".

The Hadith reported in Sunnah of Tirmidhi states that Aisha RA said that, once a man came to the Prophet SAW and sat down in front of him. Then he said that, "I have servants and slaves of mine, that they are lying to me and cheating from my wealth. They are disobeying me. So, in return, I discipline them. What will be the right between me and them?"

The Prophet SAW said that, "The amounts that they embezzled from you and the amount that they were basically dishonest, that will be accounted for. And your punishment will also be accounted for. And if your retribution was exact same as the amount of their injustice, then the situation will be neither for you or against you. However, if your punishment is more than the crimes that they had committed, then you will have to pay them back. If your punishment was less than the harm that they had done, then they will pay back to you".

So, the man became agitated and he started to tremble. He began to cry. He said, "Ya Rasool Allah SAW I'm not sure what to do?" Prophet SAW recited the Ayah of

Quran that, "We're going to bring forth the scales on the day of judgement, and no soul shall be shown any Injustice. Even if it is a mustard weight, then it will be done for them".

The man said, "O Messenger of Allah SAW, I think that the best option for me is to free these servants and slaves. So that I don't have to worry about this issue". So, he ended up freeing the slaves.

Now, the point in the hadith is that in this case, the people were doing something they should not have done. They are stealing money. And the man is administrating what was at that time their level of justice. Then the Prophet SAW is saying that there's a Justice in front of Allah SWT, and each side is going to have to measure up, and if it is exactly equal, then they are fine.

But who can be exactly equal? How can you be exactly equal? If this is the reality between the master and the slave, then how about between two people that don't have that relationship?

So, the better thing to do is not to get involved in getting an eye for an eye, and forgive for the sake of Allah SWT. Of course, this is something that is in the Quran as well that, "Whoever does an evil, should be returned with an evil. And whoever forgives, then Allah SWT will give him his reward".

Haq of Animals

We have another beautiful Hadith that our Prophet SAW said that, "On the day of judgement, every single person will give the Haq to the one who was deserving of it. Every person's Haq is going to be measured and given back. So much so, that the Sheep that did not have horns, is going to complain to Allah STW about the sheep that did have horns and butted into it".

This is something that is mentioned in the books of Tafsir. In Surah An-Naba, Allah SWT says that, "The people will say, 'Woe to me. How I wish I was dust'." These are the Kafirs. They will say this, when they see all of the animals that have finished their Hisab between them, and they will then be turned into dust.

The point being that, Allah SWT's infinite and perfect justice even manifest itself upon animals. That if an animal did something to another animal, even they will be held responsible. This also proves that animals, they have the capacity to do things that are unjust as well.

Our scholars point out that this is a very interesting example. The zebra will not complain to Allah SWT that the lion ate it. Because the lion had the right to hunt and eat the zebra.

Now, what is going to be their equivalent of heaven and hell? It's none of our concern and it is something that we leave it to Allah SWT. What we need to be extra careful about our own rights.

Two Types of Sin

Now, it is very clear that sins are of two types. There are those sins that are between you and Allah SWT. They don't harm or hurt or affect anybody else. If you're lax in your rituals, if you are doing something in your private life, like drugs, alcohol, or Zina; these are the types of sins between you and Allah SWT. This is a personal matter and Allah SWT shall forgive, if you turn to him in forgiveness.

However, if you have done harm to another person, stolen money, or beaten, physically harmed, brought pain, or anguish for no reason, or grief or slandering, or anything of this nature; then you have to worry about it.

These are two different courts. There is the court between you and Allah SWT. You have to repent for that. Then there is the special court, that is called the court of Iqtisas between people. That's why, our Prophet SAW said, "Fear injustice. Because injustice shall be turned into darkness on the day of judgement".

Worst Injustice

Of course, what is the worst that a person can do to another person? Obviously, it is the Zulm of murder, of taking the soul without a just cause. That is why, our Prophet SAW said, "The first matter that will be judged between people, on the day of judgment, will be with regards to any bloodshed that has taken place".

In one Hadith ibn Abbas RA said that, the Prophet SAW said, "The one who was murdered, shall drag his murder on the day of judgement, holding him by his forelock. Holding him with complete control. And the wounds that were caused are still going to be gushing blood out. And he will go in front of Allah SWT with the Murderer and he will say, 'Ya Rab, ask this man why did he kill me'. Until he will be brought forth all the way next to the Throne of Allah SWT. He will be given Prime status".

Our Prophet SAW said, "There should always be hope for a person on the day of judgment, as long as he doesn't shed the blood of somebody else". This is a warning to all those around the world, who are helping tyrannical regimes, those who are in charge of torturing prisoners, those who are the elite bodyguards of those that have been commanded to hurt and harm and to kill other people.

Fear that day. What will you do, when that innocent lady, when that child, when that man drags you to Allah

SWT for his Justice? What will you do, when they hold on to your head and you will have no power? What will you do, when you are going to dragged in front of the Throne of Allah SWT, directly in front of Allah SWT? That's why our Prophet SAW said, "Be careful of that injustice in particular".

There's a Hadith of Prophet SAW that, a man will come holding on to another man's hand and he will say, "Oh my Rab this person killed me". So, Allah SWT will ask him, "Why did you kill this man?" The man will say, "I did It for the glory of the one I was taking orders from". Meaning is the who commanded him. Which can be the king, the powerful person, the minister etc.

The Allah SWT will say, "The glory does not belong to that person. It belongs to Allah SWT". Then, all of the sin that the murdered man would have in his life, all of that will be transferred to the murderer. On top of that, the murderer has the sin of the murder itself.

So, the murdered person will die as Shaheed, and then the Murderer will get the whole lifetime of the sins of the first person. So, how foolish is the person and how evil is the person who does not understand the sin of this grave injustice of murder.

How to Make it Halal

Now, as mentioned before, our Prophet SAW said, "Who wherever has done any Injustice to his brother, let him make it Halal. Let him get rid of it in this world". The question is, how does one do that?

There are many ways. The first and most obvious way is, to go up to that person and to apologize and to confess for your mistake, and ask for their forgiveness, and ask Allah to forgive them for forgiving you. So, you have to apologies for if you have physically hurt a person. Or for slandering, back biting, stealing money etc.

Now, it is possible that the first person will not accept your apology. They may say that they want you to go back to the gathering that you insulted them in and praise them there. That's a very valid condition. And he has the right to do that.

Or the man can say, "You stole you my money. Before I forgive you, you need to repay that to the best of your ability, then I will forgive". So, any reasonable demand should be met.

If the demand is unreasonable, then obviously, Allah SWT does not burden a soul with more than it can bear. For example, if the person demands that for the $1,000 that were stolen, he wants $10,000 in return. It doesn't work that way. You just pay back the stolen $1,000 and ask for forgiveness.

So, if the first person is unreasonable, then the one who has done injustice, should be reasonable and give back whatever is reasonable to give. The rest is up to Allah SWT. This is the ideal situation and scenario.

Now, if you cannot find the person, or it would cause more damage to go to the person by bringing up the past, or the person that you did the damage to has passed away, or the person that you did the damage to is not an individual rather a group, institution or corporation etc.; in this case, you must make it up in a generic manner. You do that by giving some charity on behalf of those whom you have done any wrong to.

Suppose you said something about somebody, that you shouldn't have said, and you hurt that person's feelings. Then that person passed away. So then, you should do some good deeds on their behalf. So, you make your own mind, and every person is different. You have to answer to Allah SWT.

You make a fine or a penalty in your mind. That for example, the penalty for speaking ill of a person deserves $1000. You should give this in charity on behalf of that person. And you say to Allah SWT that all of this money that you are giving to the poor, the reward of this should go to so-and-so, because of what you have done.

Now, question arises, what if you cannot even do that? Or the crime is so great that no amount of apology can make up for it? That you have gone beyond the red line and it doesn't matter whether you apologize or not. You have done too much.

A simple example, these evil people around the world, that are basically minions of tyrannical regimes, and they are obeying the call of those who tell them to kill and torture; what if one of them repents? Let's say, the person was in charge of the interrogation. Nauzubillah, a very evil person.

These types of people, they have sold their Deen and their Dunya, both for the sake of this Dunya. That is the worst transaction to make. They sold everything they had, for a cheap sum of this world only.

So, imagine, one of them, after years and years of torture of innocent people; he then decides to repent. Now, his crimes are far too much to simply go knocking on the family's door and apologize.

In this case, it does appear from the text of the Quran and Sunnah, that Allah SWT will look at the quality of the repentance. Allah SWT will look at the sincerity of the repentance. If that repentance was genuine, and sincere, and powerful, then even this person can be forgiven.

The evidence for this is in the Quran and Sunnah. The generality of the verses that talk about the forgiveness of the people who repent to Allah SWT. Specifically, Allah SWT says, "Those who are torturing the believing men and women, and then do not repent, they shall be in the punishment of the fire of hell". So, this Ayah is very explicit. It means that if they repented, then they are forgiven.

Also, we have a hadit in Sahih Bukhari, of the man who killed 99 people. A very evil mass murderer. Then he decided to repent to Allah SWT. Then he killed another person. Then, finally, he made a sincere repentance and he turned to Allah SWT, and he passed away in that state of mind. According to the Hadith, he was in fact forgiven.

Now, we can understand that the sincere and genuine person can be forgiven. How about those 100 people that were killed? How about them? Why will they not get their Haq?

The general rule is that, the one who does wrong, will have to pay from his own personal account of good deeds. If he runs out of good deeds, the bad deeds of the person will be given to him.

However, if a person is sincere to the core; in this case, it appears that, Allah SWT will directly reward those whom he harmed, those whom he killed, those whom he irritated. Allah SWT will take care of them from his own self. And the man is not going to have to give, if and only if, the repentance was completely sincere.

This is also proven in the Hadith in Sahih Bukhari. Abu Huraira RA narrated that the Prophet SAW said, "Allah STW laughs at two people. One of them kills the other, and both of them end up in Jannah".

Abu Huraira RA said, "How is that possible, that the killer and the killed, they both end up as friends in Jannah?" The prophet SAW gave the example that, "A person was fighting for the sake of Allah SWT and he died a Shaheed. He's going to go to Jannah. The one who killed him from the side of the enemy, he's not upon the religion of Allah SWT. Eventually Allah SWT guides him to Islam. Then he as well dies a Shaheed. So, both of them are brothers in Jannah".

This is very explicit here that Zulm can be eased with a very sincere repentance. If and only if, the person who did the Zulm, for whatever reason, is not able to repay all of that back to the one whom he has done Zulm to.

Chronology of Iqtisas

Now, the question arises, when and where will this occur? Will it occur on the plane of the day of judgement? Will it occur on the bridge, or before the bridge, or after the bridge? Or before entering Heaven or Hell?

Now there will be a bridge on the day of Judgement called Qantara. It is different from Sirat, which is another bridge on the day of Judgement.

Qantara is typically a U-shaped bridge, that is put in front of the fortified walls, that comes on over the water or the moat, and connects the land with the fort. It is lifted to prevent un authorized people, or invading armies from entering the fort.

It is as if, Jannah has that fortress wall. And to get in to the wall of Jannah, you have to pass by this massive bridge. It is after the Sirat.

Some Hadiths mention that this whole back-and-forth between people it will take place on the Qantara. Of those is the Hadith in Bukhari that, once the Believers have guaranteed that they're not going to hell, they're marching on the way to Jannah, after the Hisab, and they have got their scrolls.

Then they shall be prevented or stopped at the Qantara between heaven and hell. Then they shall swap any

Zulm that they have done to each other. They shall deal with them at this point in time. Until finally when they have been purified and cleansed, when everything has been done between them, it will then be allowed for them to enter Jannah.

Then Prophet SAW said, "I swear to you that, every one of them will inherently know how to get to their place in Jannah. Just like every one of you knows how to get to their home in your city".

Now, this obviously raises some issues. Of them is that, the very Hadith of the one who is bankrupt says that, he shall have mountains of good deeds. But after all of this is over, he shall enter into the fire of hell. So, this hadith suggest that Iqtisas is taking place at the Hisab.

There are other Hadiths as well, that seem to indicate that there are two separate courts. One for rights of Allah SWT and the other for the rights of people. The Prophet SAW said, the first matter for which Hisab will be made between the servant and his Lord is the Salah. And the first matter for which Hisab will be made between the people will be for blood".

Ibn Hajar RA he comments on this and says, "How come the Iqtisas is placed right before Jannah? Of what use is it, when the people already know they're going to Jannah?" So, he says that, this Iqtisas between the people of Jannah is going to be for the ranks of Jannah. It's not going to be to go to Jahannam.

Al Qurtubi RA, he brings a weak narration, that there are seven bridges or Qantara before Jannah. And at every single Qantara, a different series of questions are going to be asked. One of these questions will be for Iqtisas.

Now, those people who are going to end up in Jahannam, they will not wait till the very end of the Qantara. They will not wait till after the Sirat. Because those who passed the Sirat, they're going to Jannah. They are not going to be dragged back down into Jahannam.

Therefore, the criminals and the evil people, that have harmed other people of humanity and who are destined to go to Jahannam, those people, they shall have their Hisab and their Iqtisas all done together on the plains of the day of judgment.

So, as they're standing in front of Allah SWT for their Hisab, simultaneously, their sins between them and Allah SWT, and their sins between them and the creation shall be accounted for. Then they shall end up in the fire of Hell.

However, there will be those, who they overall have enough good deeds to make it in to Jannah. But they have wronged other people. Subhan Allah, every single human being amongst us, we have wronged other people. We have not been perfect in our lives. Those people, they will get the verdict that you're going to Jannah. But they're not going to get in until the very final details of the Hisab are done.

This is the Iqtisas between the people. What is the purpose now of the good and bad deeds, when you're going to enter Jannah? It appears, and Allah knows best, that there's going to be a reshuffling of levels of Jannah. That's the only thing that is left.

That right before the entrance of Jannah, the people of Jannah will be waiting outside. Then for example, a person going in to a higher level of Jannah had wronged a person going in to a lower level of Jannah, then after Iqtisas, the other person will be going in to a better level of Jannah then before.

Mizan

Now, this is another aspect that is very explicit in the Quran and in the Sunnah. It is mentioned on numerous occasions in our sacred text. Many of our treatises about theology and about Aqedah, mention Mizan as a part of our fundamentals. That in order to be a faithful Muslim, you need to believe in this concept of the Mizan, or the scales on the day of Judgement.

Now the word Mizan, it means the Scales. The Quran and Sunnah are very explicit with this word. It has been used over a dozen or two dozen times in all of the Hadiths that mentioned the concept of the scales.

The concept of the scales is something that would occur most likely after the Hisab and after the scrolls. Even though there is no explicit chronology of events. But that is the opinion of the scholars.

What does the word Mizan mean? The word Mizan comes from the Arabic word Wazana. Wazana means Weight. The classical meaning according to the lexicon authors is that Wazana does not only means your actual weight, but it also implies your status, and your merit, and it also implies justice. Mizan is the noun of the instrument that is used to do Wazana, or the instrument that is used to weigh.

One of the unique things that really makes the Arabic language stand out is the conjugation of verbs. The fact that one verb can be conjugated to over 200 structures. Then those morphological structures will pattern you to extract dozens, if not hundreds of words from that rood verb. This is unique to the Semitic languages.

The word Mizan, it actually comes from the morphological structure that indicates the instrument that is used to do the weight.

That's one of the reasons why, Arabic is very powerful and beautiful, that you can take a verb, and permutate it and conjugate from it, literally dozens of verbs, if not actually more than this.

Symbol of Justice

Of course, it is well known that a scale has been used from the beginning of times. The instrument of the scale, itself has symbolized justice from the very beginning of time. In fact, even in our Western cultures, if you go to a courthouse, generally speaking, you will find a blindfolded person, carrying the scales.

The notion of the scales being used to symbolize impartially weighing the evidence and serving justice, is not just in the Quran. It is something that is found in many traditions and cultures.

In fact, even in the ancient Babylonian textbooks, and in the famous Egyptian book called the Book of The Dead of the Pharaonic Religion, this notion is found. The ancient Egyptians, they had a religion and their religion is preserved in something called the Book of The Dead. That's their holy book.

In this Book of the Dead, there actually are images of a goddess that they had, that is carrying the scales of justice. That notion eventually transformed into Roman times. Where they had a goddess that they called the goddess of justice, and it was a lady who would have scales. In Roman times, the goddess of justice would have a temple and shrine.

That notion trickled down to Christianity. Which trickled down to Europe. Then around the 12th or 13th century, we begin to see this notion of a lady that is blindfolded, and is carrying the scales, and is symbolizing justice.

Mizan in Other Traditions

Now, what if somebody were to say that Quran mentions scales as justice, and it's found in Babylonian traditions, it's found in Egyptian traditions, it is found in ancient Christianity; therefore, in fact Quran is the same motif as all of these other traditions.

The answer to this is very straight forward, and this is the response that I've also given, when people have asked me about the flood of Noah and the Great Flood. That the concept of a great flood is found in every single tradition in the world.

There is not a single civilization, except that it has a notion of a flood. In fact, not only ancient creation myths in Babylon, not only in ancient Egypt, but even when the anthropologist first came across the Aborigines populations of Australia, and the anthropologist studied the Aborigines, they came across the story of a great flood.

So, very simple response to the question is that, we flip it around 180 degrees. We can say that, the very fact that all of these civilizations have a flood story, indicates that there was in fact a great flood at some point in history. Therefore, all these civilizations preserved that notion of a great flood.

Similarly, the fact that justice is symbolized with scales in Islam and other civilization is because Allah SWT revealed this concept to all of them. In fact, it is mentioned in the Quran very explicit in the Quran that, "We shall place the scales as a sign of justice".

The fact that the Quran mentions it, and is mentioned in the ancient Egyptian text etc., all that it indicates is that this has been from the beginning of humanity, that Allah SWT in the earliest of earlier religions, he revealed this concept. Therefore, it remained embedded in the human psyche and sub consciousness, until we find it in all of these different cultures that are non-Islamic and we find it in the Quran as well.

Scales in the Quran

Now, the Quran and Sunnah are very explicit about affirming the concept of Mizan. For example, in Surah Al-A'raf, Allah SWT says that, "On that day, the weighing on that day is going to happen with truth" Allah SWT says in Surah Al-Anbiya verse 47, "We shall place the scales of justice on the day of judgement"

So, Allah SWT is mentioning that on day of judgment, there is going to be scales, and these scales will symbolize and will execute justice.

In Surah Al-Qaryat, the Quran mentions the scales being heavy and the scales being light. This concept is mentioned in four or five verses in the Quran. In Surah Al-Mu'minun Allah SWT says, "Whoever's scales are heavy, they shall be successful. Whoever's scales are light, they shall be in Jahannam to abide therein forever". So, we have here the concept of heavy and light scales.

In Surah Kahf, Allah SWT says, "Those people who rejected Allah SWT and disbelieved in him, their good deeds are destroyed. So, we shall not establish for them the weight of scales on the day of Judgement". The fact that they have been negated to have weight, because they have rejected Allah SWT, indicates that those who believe in Allah SWT are going to have that weight with the scales on the day of Judgement.

If we gather just the Quranic verses, it is quite clear that the scales are real. This negates metaphor. If somebody were to say the scales are indicative. That the scales are symbolic of Allah SWT's justice. To that we say, the fact that Allah SWT explicitly says, "We are going to bring it with Haq", therefore it negates symbolism.

The Scales are not symbolic. The Scales are real on the day of Judgement. They are meant for justice. They are actual scales that are going to come on the day of Judgement.

Also, the fact that Allah SWT says, "The scale will be heavy, and if they are heavy, the person will be successful. The scale will be light and if it is light, they will not be successful". This all indicates the realities of the scales.

Scales in Hadith Literature

As for the Hadith literature, there are a number of very explicit hadith about Scales. Some of them are authentic. Some of them not so authentic.

Of the most authentic hadith and of the most famous Hadith about the concept of scales, is the hadith in Sahih Buhari, in the chapter of establishing the scales on the day of Judgement. It is the very last hadith of Buhari. It says, "Two are the phrases, that are very light on the tongue and very heavy on the scales and very beloved to Allah SWT. Subhan Allahi Wabi-Habdihi, Subhan Allahil Azeem".

Imam Bukhari RA ends his book with the concept of actions and deeds. Having pure intentions is not good enough. You have to act on those intentions as will.

In fact, in one hadith in Musnad Imam Ahmed, the mention of scales is actually listed in the famous hadith of what is Iman and what is Islam.

The Hadith is that, a Sahabi asked the Prophet SAW, "O Messenger of Allah SWT, what is Iman?" Our Prophet SAW responded, "Iman is to believe in Allah STW, and the last day, and Angels, and the books, and the Prophets AS, and to believe in death, and life after death, and heaven and hell, and the Hisab, and the

Mizan, and to believe in all of Qadr. The good of it, and the bad of it".

So, the man said, "If I believe in all of this, am I a believer?" The Prophet SAW said, "Yes, you are". So, in this Hadith on one of the six pillars of Iman, he mentions a longer list, and in that list, he specifically mentions to believe in the Mizan.

Also, in the famous Hadith of Sahih Muslim, our Prophet SAW said, "Doing Wudu is half of Iman". Meaning, whoever is concerned with Wudu and doing Wudu all the time, and praying regularly; that is half of your Iman.

Then the Prophet SAW says, "And saying Alhamdulillah, it fills the scales on the day of Judgement. And 'Subhan Allah, Wal-Hamdulillah' fills up all that is between the heavens and the earth. And the prayer is a light, and the charity is an evidence. And being patient shall be an illuminating force. And the Quran is either an evidence for you or against you".

This beautiful Hadith explicitly says that, saying Alhamdulillah fills the scales. So, one Alhamdulillah said from the depths of the heart and acted upon it, will fill the Scales.

So once again, he is affirming there's something called the scales. He's affirming that good deeds are going to be in the scales. And he's affirming that good deeds are not all of the same size.

Some good deeds are bigger than others, and of the biggest of deeds is the Zikr of Allah SWT. And our Prophet SAW is saying that one small phrase makes the scales heavy. So, Zikr of Allah SWT is something very important to have for the Scales.

In the Hadith of Sunnah Tirmidhi, our Prophet SAW said, "There is nothing that is heavier in the scales on the day of Judgement Day than having good manners". So, once again, we have this notion of good deeds being heavy in the Scales.

Our Prophet SAW is encouraging specific good deeds, in order to have heavy Scales. So, we had better be paying attention. We had better be contemplating that these aren't just abstract notions. We should act on them. Our Prophet SAW is specifically mentioning Zikr and also good manners. Nothing is heavier than good manners on the scales of the day of Judgement.

In another hadith in Musnad of Imam Ahmed with a slightly weak chain, our Prophet SAW said, "What will make you understand, that five are the things; how heavy they are on the Scales. La Ilaha Il Allah, Allahu Akbar, Subhan Allah, Alhamdulillah, and then the death of a righteous child and the parents are patient at the passing of the child". So, this is again a very explicit hadith about the issue of good deeds being put in the scales.

There's a very beautiful narration in the Sunnah of Abu Dawood in the chapter of the Scales. Aisha RA says that, one day she thought of the fire of Hell and began to cry. The Prophet SAW visited her at that time. Fe said, "what is causing you to cry?"

Aisha RA said, "I remembered the fire of hell and I began to cry. O Messenger of Allah SAW, will you remember your family on the day of Judgement?"

The Prophet SAW said, "Three are the times, no person will remember another person. number one, is Mizan. When the scales are placed, and until a person knows if his scales are heavy or not. Number two, at the time of the handing of the scrolls. Until the person knows which hand is his scroll going to be put in. The right hand, or the left hand, or from behind him. Number 3, when the bridge is placed over Jahannam, and you have to cross that bridge".

Description of Mizan

Now, what are the descriptions of Mizan? Well, when it comes to describing the Mizan, the fact of the matter is that, the Quran and the Sunnah are silent on the details. We do have what are called statements, from students of the Shaba, from the second and third generation.

We find in the earliest books ever written about theology, some descriptions about Scales. But to the best of my knowledge, there is no explicit hadith of the Prophet SAW, that's authentic, that describes the scale.

So, in our earliest of books, there was this notion that the scale is going to have two sides to it. Of course, this is how the common weigh scales are.

It is also mentioned in some of these books that Jibril AS will come with the scales, or he shall be carrying the scales. It is mentioned that the scale, one side of it will be on the side of Jannah, and one side will be on the side of Jahannam. So, if the Jannah side becomes heavier, person is going to Jannah.

We also know that the scale will be placed in front of the throne of Allah SWT. On the right will be Jannah, on the left will be Jahannam.

We also have this notion that one side of the scale shall have a light shining on it and the other will be dark. So, the good deeds will be in the light side. Therefore, if it is heavy, everybody will see. And if it is light, everybody will see. All of these notions, they are not found in an explicit hadith that are authentic, to the best of my knowledge.

Part of Our Creed

Now, the most famous treatise of our theology ever written in the history of Islam, it is Al-Tahawi RA's creed. But we always have to remember that the creed of Al-Tahawi RA is not from Allah SWT. It is something that a great scholar in the 4th century of the hijra wrote. He died in 310 AD. So, a great scholar of the 4th century compiled what he believes is the creed, and he places it in this book.

Do realize that it is a great attempt. It is a blessed attempt. No other book on creed has been accepted across the spectrum of those who believe in the Sunnah like Al-Tahawi RA's creed. But remember it is not revealed from Allah SWT. And there are other creeds that have been written by scholars interested in the Sunnah as well.

Now, if you look at those early creeds, and there are many in number. They have been continued to be written up until our times. Many of them explicitly list the principles of Iman. One of them is that we believe in the Mizan. And Al-Tahawi RA explicitly affirms the Mizan.

Other authorities of earliest Islam, including Ibn Battah RA and Abul Hasan al Ashari RA and Al-Lalakai RA, and so many others of our early scholars of Islam, have written books about Islamic creed, all the way down to As-Safarini RA.

As-Safarini RA who died 300 years ago, wrote a very famous book about creed. It also is a very comprehensive book. He says that part of our creed is that we must believe in the Mizan.

Is Mizan Metaphorical

Did any Muslim group deny the Mizan? it is mentioned that one strand of the pseudo rationalist they're called Mu'tazila, they said the Mizan is metaphorical for justice, and that there is not an actual Mizan. It's not going to be actual physical scales.

They dismissed the Hadith, because they did not follow the Hadith. They interpreted the Quran to mean that, whenever Allah STW says, "We shall place the scales of justice", they said that the references is to justice and not the scales.

But as we explained, the Quran and the Sunnah are simply too explicit to be metaphorical. So, Allah SWT knows best. All of the scholars disagree with their metaphorical interpretation.

Imam Safarini RA says that, "The tradition has explicitly mentioned that the Mizan is a real Scale. That it has two sides. That it has a middle pillar". This is the position of Ibn Abbas RA and Hasan al-Basri RA. And he says that, "There is unanimous consensus upon the people of truth of the Muslims, that we believe in a literal Mizan"

Chronology of Mizan

Now, the chronology of the events of the day of Judgement is not set in stone. So, the question arises, when will the Mizan be set up? Will it be set up during the Hisab, or before the Hisab, or after the Hisab?

If you look at the Quran and the Sunnah, there does not seem to be an explicit chronology about the Mizan and the Hisab. Nonetheless, Imam Al-Qurtubi RA, he has written one of the most comprehensive books about the Day of Judgement. Imam Al-Qurtubi RA says that, "The Mizan is going to occur right after the Hisab".

He bases this on the common sense notion of what exactly is the Hisab, and what exactly is the Mizan The Hisab is going to be the reckoning that will take place between Allah SWT and the person. The Mizan is the manifestation of that reckoning. Once the reckoning has been done, we need to see actual of it. So, he says logically, that the Mizan will occur after the Hisab.

Now, when will the fountain come into place? Now, many Ulema have said that the fountain of the Prophet SAW will occur after the Hisab and before the Mizan. So, there's going to be an interlude.

And many scholars have said that it is going to occur after the Mizan. But we do not know for certain.

Perhaps there is no chronological order. Perhaps everything will be happening somewhat simultaneously.

Who is Mizan for?

Now, the question arises, who is going to be subjugated to this Mizan? Is it going to be for all of mankind, or is it going to be for only those who believed in Allah SWT, and they will then be tested with the Mizan?

The majority of scholars have said that, the Mizan is only for those who claimed faith. As for those who did not claim faith, then there is no point of the Mizan. Because if they didn't believe in Allah SWT, there is no hope for them and there's no point of subjugating them to Mizan. This is the dominant opinion.

There is a small group of Ulema, including Sheikh Rashid Rida RA, who is the greatest Ulema and thinker of the last century, and he was the first global scholar while he was alive. He stated that the Mizan is for the Kafir and the Muslim. And he felt that this is Allah SWT's infinite justice.

However, Ibn Taymiyyah RA, Al Qurtubi RA, and An-Nawawi RA, and many of the earlier Ulema said that the Scales are only for the believers. By believers, it means those who said they are believers. Because many of them are not actual believers. Many of them are hypocrites. Many of them are evil, even though they have some Iman.

As for the Kafir, they said that, there is no concept of Mizan for them. They brought evidences for this. Of those evidences, Surah Kahf verse 105, which is the most explicit evidence. Allah STW says that, "Those who disbelieved in Allah SWT, their deeds have basically gone to waste, and we shall not even place for them scales on the day of Judgement".

Allah STW says in the Quran that, "All the good deeds that they sent forward, we will scatter it into dust and it will become useless". Because they didn't do something for the sake of Allah SWT. So, they shall not be rewarded by Allah STW.

So, when there are no good deeds, and when all of their good deeds have been scattered into the dust, when they didn't do something that's going to be rewarded; what is the purpose of them to have Mizan?

Ibn Taymiyyah RA writes that, "There shall be no weighing for the Kafir, because they don't have any good deeds to be weighed in the first place. The weighing is only for the believers. The impious and the pious. They are going to be the ones that will be weighed. The impious of the believers, their scales will be light. Then they shall go to Jahannam".

Now this is an interpretation. At the same time, other Scholars, they argue alternative positions. Of those positions is the Ayah of Surah Mu'minun. The context of

Surah Mu'minun is talking about the Kafir and the Mumin. So, it is as if there's an indication that there might indeed be a Scale for them. But the Kafir will have light scales.

What Will Be Put on The Scales?

Now, what will be put on the scales on the day of Judgement? What exactly will be placed inside the scales? We have actually three opinions, and all these opinions have some evidence. Once again, there's no practical implication of the actual difference, and doesn't really change the end result.

Three things are mentioned. The first of them is the most minority opinion. In fact, it's pretty clear that this position is not the correct one, even though we respect those who said it. They say that the human being himself will be placed in the scales. But on that day, it's not going to weigh your physical weight, but rather the deeds.

This is actually a hadith of the Prophet SAW in Sahih Bukhari. The Prophet SAW said, "A large, fat, and very big bulky man will be brought on the day of Judgement, and he shall not weigh a mosquito's wing's wait on the day of Judgement".

Then the Prophet SAW said, "Read if you wish, the verse in the Quran, 'We will not give them any weight on the day of Judgement'". So, this hadith seems to indicate that the human being himself will be put on the scales. As our Prophet SAW is saying a large man will come, and because he did no good deeds, he will not even weigh the wings of a mosquito.

Another hadith in a number of traditions, including Sahih Muslim and Musnad Imam Ahmed, and others; that our Prophet SAW said regarding the shin of Ibn Masud RA.

So, Ibn Masud RA, he had an issue with his legs, and his legs had a curvature. He had a bit of a deformity in his legs. Once he was climbing a tree to get a miswak for brushing his teeth. Some of the younger Sahaba were sitting there. So, because he's climbing the tree, his shin became visible and they could see the curvature of the shin.

Some of them began to just laugh at that. Which is of course not good to do. Our Prophet SAW, He saw them laughing, and he said, "Do you laugh at the shin of Ibn Masud? For Wallaahi, it is heavier in the Mizan then the mountain of Uhud".

Now, this hadith firstly indicates that we should not be making fun of people. Especially, to make fun of people's appearance. Because Ibn Masud RA did not create himself. Allah SWT created him. So, to make fun of the creation, is to make fun of the creator. To make fun of how somebody looks, is to make fun of the one who put him in that way.

So that's why our Prophet SAW became angry, and he said that, "how dare you laugh", and then divert the point to, "Who are you making fun of?" He said that,

"The leg that you're laughing at, it is heavier in the scales than the mountain of Uhud".

Now what does that indicate? The Hadith Seems to indicate that Ibn Masud RA himself will be placed in the Scales and that one shin of his that they were laughing at is going to be heavier than the mountain of Uhud.

This Hadith seems to indicate that the person will be placed in the scales, and what will be weighed is not the physical weight of the person, but rather the weight of his or her good deeds.

The second opinion is that, what will be weighed is the good deed itself. The good deed will somehow transform into an icon, or an object, or an item. It will be transformed in to a physical entity that will be placed in the scales.

There are many evidences for this. Prophet SAW said, "The heaviest thing on the day of Judgement will be good manners". So, it's going to become something that will be placed in the scales.

Another evidence is the hadith is that, "Alhamdulillah fills the scales". Of the evidence is the hadith that, "Subhan Allahi Wabi-Habdihi Subhan Allahil Azeem makes the scales heavy".

The point here is that the deeds themselves will become physical, tangible realities. How? We don't know, and we don't care. Allah SWT will do it. Allah SWT will transform these entities into actual physical things that can then be placed into the scales, and each one will have a mass of its own. And certain things will be heavier than other things.

The third opinion is that the scrolls of the deeds will be placed in the Mizan. The scrolls of good deeds will be placed on the right side and the scrolls of the bad deeds will be placed on the left side. This opinion is the majority one.

It also includes the second opinion within it. Because you can also say that the scrolls that have Alhamdulillah written on it, and the good deeds that have the good manners written on it, when it is placed in the scale, it will be the heaviest thing.

Of the most explicit evidences for this, is the famous Hadith in Ibn Majah and others, that, "A man shall come with 99 scrolls of evil deeds and they shall be placed on one side of the scale, and he shall not have any good deeds. It will be said to him to go to Jahannam. Until finally, an Angel will call out that there is one deed left. And a card will come, and on that card, there will be La Ilaha Ill Allah. and that card shall be placed on the other side of the scale".

So, according to this hadith the scroll and the card of deeds is placed on the scale. And this Inshallah, it makes the most sense.

As for the hadith of the man will come, and he will be weight nothing, and the hadith about Ibn Masud RA's shin, it doesn't mean that Ibn Masud RA is going to sit in the scale. It means that, this is a person whose deeds are so weighty that even one shin of his, metaphorically speaking here, is heavier than the entire mountain of Uhud.

It means that, you don't judge people based upon their outer looks. You judge based upon their deeds. It means that no matter how big weighty you are, both physically and metaphorically, it means nothing on the day of judgement. What matters is your heart and your good deeds. And Allah SWT knows best.

Number of Mizan on Day of Judgement

Now, how many Mizan will there be? Some scholars have said that, every person will have a Mizan. Some have said there's going to be one scale for all of mankind. Some have said that there's going to be a Mizan for every single Ummah. So, we have multiple positions.

For example, Imam Safarini RA said that, "Every Ummah shall have his own scale". Hasan Al Basri RA said, "Every human being will have a special scale for him". Al Qurtubi RA said, "There's going to be one scale that is going to be used by all of mankind". In the end of the day, Allah SWT knows best. It is not that we are obliged to believe in a specific quantity of scales.

The purpose of Mizan is to demonstrate tangibly, in a manner that our eyes can see, to show and to demonstrate Allah SWT's infinite justice.

Now, what if the scales come and they are exactly equal in weight? The response is that the Hadith does not mention and the Quran does not mention explicitly what is going to happen, if the scales are absolutely even. The reality is that, for these types of scenarios, there is nothing mentioned.

Hawd of Prophet SAW

Now, the next major topic for the day of Judgement, is the very beautiful and interesting topic of the fountain, or the pool, or the cistern of our Prophet SAW; which is known as the Hawd.

The Day of Judgement, as we know, is going to be a very difficult day and it is going to be a day that is very hot. As the Hadith mentioned that, "The sun is going to come close, until it is just one mile away. There's going to be no shade on that day, except the shade that Allah SWT chooses to give to the people. People will be sweating profusely. So much so that, some people's sweat will go up till their shins. Others will go to their thighs. Others will go all the way to their necks".

Meaning that, people will be sweating because of that heat. Therefore, we need to drink water. And how will the righteous drink on that day? On that day, there shall be only one source of water. That source is the fountain, or the pool of the Prophet SAW, that is called the Hawd.

The Hawd in Arabic means the cistern or the pool. By pool it means something that is raised up. So. it is going to be something that is like a water canister, that you store water in. Something that when the travelers, when they come, they drink from it. That's called the Hawd.

So, there is going to be a large water cistern or a water canister on the day of judgement for the people of Iman to drink water from. It is going to be massive pool to store water and that people can walk up to, and then there will be cups there and they can drink from it. This is called the Hawd of our Prophet SAW.

Al-Kawthar

Now this Hawd, it is not mentioned in the Quran. However, the Quran mentions the Kawthar in Surah Al-Kawthar. And the Kawthar is the source of the water of the Hawd.

So, what is the Kawthar? The Kawthar is one of the main rivers of Jannah that has been gifted to our Prophet SAW. It is described with beautiful imagery. That the banks of the Kawthar are carved out pearls. That its water is colder than ice, and more fragrant than perfume, and sweeter than honey.

This is the first taste that the people on the day of Judgement will get of Jannah, will be those Muslims who are drinking from the Hawd; who's water comes from the Kawthar.

The people on the day of Judgement have not yet entered Jannah. And the first taste they will get of Jannah, will be when they drink from the pool, whose source is going to be the river of Jannah, and that is the Kawthar.

Part of Our Creed

Now, the Kawthar is mentioned in the Quran. The Hawd is not mentioned in the Quran. But it is mentioned in the prophetic traditions. It is one of those traditions, that has reached the level of Mutawatir.

Mutawatir means a Hadith that has been narrated by so many people, that there is no doubt of its certainty. It is established beyond doubt that our Prophet SAW has said and told us about the Hawd.

Furthermore, some scholars have compiled this tradition. Ibn Hajar RA, he comments that, Al-Qa'deyat RA has listed 25 companions of Prophet SAW, who have narrated about the Hawd of the Prophet SAW.

Imam An-Nawawi RA, who came after Al-Qa'deyat RA, he added three more people to that list, to get 28 people in total. Then Ibn Hajar RA says that, "And I found an equivalent number to all of them". Thus, making the total number of companions to narrate the Hawd more than 50.

He says that from these 50 companions, there are almost 100 chains that are talking about the Hawd of the Prophet SAW. Therefore, these hadiths telling us about the fountain, it has reached the highest level of authenticity, which is called Mutawatir. It is because of this, that belief in the fountain has become a point of creed for the people of Ahel Al Sunnah.

Imam Safarini RA wrote a very comprehensive book of theology around 300 years ago. He writes in this book that both the Hawd and the Kawthar are affirmed by the texts and by the unanimous consensus of all of Sunni Islam. So much so, he says that, it is now considered a fundamental part of faith. And whoever denies it becomes a person of deviation or a person of heresy.

Waiting at The Hawd

The most famous hadith about Hawd is the one in Bukhari and Muslim, that Uqba ibn Amir RA narrated that, once the Prophet SAW Prayed for the people of Uhud. Then he turned to the Sahaba, and he said, "I am going to be at the Hawd on the day of Judgement waiting for my Ummah".

The word used in the hadith in Arabic, it means the person who goes ahead of the caravan or the group, to prepare the way for the group to come. This is a technical term. The word means, the Prophet SAW is the scout who goes forward, and then he prepares.

So, imagine a caravan will go camping somewhere. Then a person is going to be there before, and clear the path, and make sure there's an area to camp, and camp is where the water is.

So, the Prophet SAW is saying, 'I will be that leader for you, that's preparing on the day of Judgement. I'm going to make sure that things are good for you. I'm going to make sure that the fountain is ready for you. And I will meet you at the Hawd".

The Hadid goes on that, "I have been given of the keys to the treasures of this world. And by Allah SWT, I am not scared that you will do Shirk after me. What I'm scared is that you will compete with one another for this world".

Meaning, the bulk of the Ummah will not fall into Shirk. The Prophet SAW is not worried that they will fall into idolatry. He is worried that they will become too greedy and they will fight one another for this world, and they will become greedy for the pleasures of this world.

Not Deserving of the Hawd

Ibn Masud reported that the Prophet SAW said, Hadith is in Bukhari and Muslim that, "I will be the one that will be waiting for you at the fountain. And groups of people will be presented to me. And I will call out to them. But then they will be snatched away from me. I will argue it, and I will say, 'Oh my Lord, these are my companions'. But then it will be said to me, 'You do not know what they changed after you. You do not know that they turned around and they left after you. They literally abandoned after you'".

So, this Hadith tells us that there will be people that the Prophet SAW recognizes as Muslims, and he is calling out to them, but the Angels will come and say, "No, these people do not deserve the Hawd".

The Effects of Wudu

And there are numerous traditions that, the Prophet SAW will recognize his Ummah on the day of Judgement from the effects of Wudu. In the Hadith of Abu Huraira RA, the Prophet SAW was asked that, "O Messenger of Allah SAW, how shall you recognize the Muslims on the day of Judgement?"

And he SAW said that, "My Ummah will come with bright faces and their limbs will be shining bright because of the effects of Wudu". So, the one who does Wudu constantly, frequently, perfectly, the one who is conscientious in doing Wudu; that is the person that should be recognized by the Prophet SAW on the day of Judgement.

The Two Mizaban

We also learnt in the Hadith of Muslim that, our Prophet SAW was asked about the fountain and he said, "The water that is in it, it is whiter than milk. And it will be sweeter than honey. There will be two Mizaban that are coming from Jannah."

A Mizab is like a long pipe. When you go to the Kaaba, one side of the Kaaba has that funnel or that pipe on its roof. That is called Mizab. Mizab is something that was used in those days to collect the water from the roof and cause it to fall down. Even in our cultures, we have various things that do that. But in the old days there was just a spout coming out that was going to collect the water and let it go down.

So, the Prophet SAW said that, "From Jannah, there will be two spouts that are coming onto the plains of the day of Judgement. One of them will be made of gold, and the other one will be made of silver. And from these two spouts, there will be the water that is coming from the Kawthar. And it will be coming into the Hawd".

Imagine and visualize this. We have the fountain, the Hawd and the source of that water will be from Jannah itself. Where there will be two spouts coming from Jannah. One made out of gleaming silver, other made out of beautiful gold. And from the Kawthar, will be coming the water into the Hawd.

Therefore, the first taste of Jannah on the day of Judgement, before getting in to Jannah, will be for those who drink from the Hawd.

How to Find the Hawd

There is a beautiful icon, or symbol, that we will be able to see when we're trying to find the Hawd. Our Prophet SAW said, the hadith is in Sahih Bukhari, "What is between my house and between my pulpit, it is one of the gardens of Paradise. And my pulpit shall be stationed at my Hawd".

So, the pulpit of the Prophet SAW will then be brought, and you will see the pulpit of the Prophet SAW as an icon that will be in front of the fountain of the Prophet SAW.

Some of our Scholars have mentioned that the symbolism here is powerful, and that is that, for those who didn't see him, like us; whoever was eager to listen to the Prophet SAW in this world, or to follow his Sunnah, or those who paid attention to what was said on the Minbar, meaning the Hadith, and the sunnah; those will be the ones, that will be guided to the Hawd, and they will be drinking from the Hawd.

In other words, your eagerness in following the Sunnah is what will cause you to drink from the Hawd. May Allah SWT make us amongst them.

Will Other Prophets AS have a Hawd?

Now, the Prophet SAW will have a Hawd on the day of Judgement. Will all the Prophets AS have a Hawd? There is a hadith in Sunnah Tirmidhi that the Prophet SAW said that, "Every Nabi has Hawd. And all the Prophets AS will be competing with one another to see who has the largest amount of people coming to his fountain. And I am optimistic that I will be the one that has the largest people of his Ummah".

Now, this hadith does have a slight weakness to it. There is basically a very slight missing link in the chain of Narration. Nonetheless, the concept seems to be valid, and that is because many of our early scholars, they consider this to be a part of our theology that all the Prophets AS have a Hawd.

Also, when our Prophet SAW listed things that are unique to him, and that have not been given to other Prophets AS, he never listed the Hawd as being unique to him. Had it been unique to him, he would have listed it.

The fact that he didn't list it, shows that every Prophet AS will have a Hawd and every Prophet AS will be calling his Ummah to his Hawd. And our Prophet SAW will be calling us to his Hawd. And He SAW would recognize us by those who perform Wudu.

Parenthetically, this is a huge warning to those who are lazy in their prayers and those who do not do Wudu. That from the beginning, from the very start of day of judgement, things are going to go downhill. So, guard your prayer and guard your Wudu. Because you want things to go uphill in the next World.

Size of The Hawd

What are some of the characteristics of the Hawd that we are familiar with? A number of things are mentioned. The first thing that is mentioned, and this is mentioned in almost every single hadith, is the massive size of the Hawd.

It is very huge and different versions of Hadith mentioned different city names to give an understanding of its approximate size. The Prophet SAW would mention typically two cities, and he would say that, length of one side of the Hawd is from city A to city B.

So, in one Hadith in Buhari, he said that, "My Hawd is between Ayla and Sana". Ayla is a city that is now in between Jordan and in the occupied lands in that region. It's a small city. Which is also a coastal city. And it goes from there, all the way to Sana in Yemen.

In another Hadith in Sahih Muslim, He SAW said, "From Ayla to Aden". Aden is also in Yemen. In another Hadith, he said, "From Medina to Sana". in another Hadith, He said, "From Aden to Oman". In another Hadith, "From Sana to Basra". And yet in another hadith, he said, "From the Kaaba to Bait Al Maqdis".

And there are many other narrations. One of the scholars has compiled all of these narrations, and has extracted 15 different combinations of cities. Whereas one hadith does not mention two cities. It mentions a time frame.

Hadith is in Sahih Muslim. The Prophet SAW said, "My fountain, it is the distance of one month's journey travelling one side of it".

Now, some people have caused doubts to come about the Sunnah by saying that all these different narrations are conflicting with one another. But in reality, there is no conflict. Our Prophet SAW is mentioning the Hawd in many Hadiths to many different people. And he's giving a rough estimate of its size. And all of these are basically a very large Areas.

Imagine the entire Arabian Peninsula of about like 2500 kilometers or 1500 miles. That's the length of just one side of the Hawd. That's how large it is.

Shape of the Hawd

Also, we learn that Hawd is in shape of a square. The Hawd is not to circle. It is a square. In the Hadith in Sahih Muslim, the Prophet SAW said, "And the sides of it are all equidistant" The only way that can happen is if you have a square.

This is actually beneficial for us, because had it been a circle, then the perimeter of the Hawd would have decreased. The square has the maximum perimeter of any type of object. Which means the maximum number of people Can drink from it.

Can you imagine a square that is 2500 kilometers on each side? That's like 10,000 kilometers. Can you imagine how many people can drink from it simultaneously, at any given time? There's going to be hundreds of millions of people that will be able to drink from the Hawd at any given time.

And then once they drink, they can go, and others can come and come. So, the Hawd is a massive, massive place, where millions and millions of people can simultaneously drink. And it is going to be in the shape of a square.

Other Characteristics of Hawd

Now, what will they drink from it? How will they get to the water inside of it? Will they use their hands? Our Prophet SAW said, Hadith is in Sahih Bukhari, "The number of cups of this fountain is just like the number of stars".

Which means they are beyond count. So, anybody who goes up to the Hawd, and gets there, you will have a cup waiting for you, and you can use that cup, and you can drink from the Hawd.

What will be inside of it? Well, because the source is the Kawthar, our Prophet SAW described the Kawthar and he described the Hawd with the exact same terminology.

In Sahih Muslim, he said, "Its water is whiter than milk, and it smell is better than perfume". In the other hadith, he SAW said, "It is sweeter than honey". In the Hadith Musnad Imam Ahmed, he SAW said, "It is colder than ice itself".

So, imagine a delectable delight. A drink that is not necessarily water. It is something that is of the of the drinks of Jannah. So, it is beyond our description. But these words, they give us a type of understanding of what it is.

Of course, when you are drinking from Jannah, what do you think one of the characteristics is going to be? Hadith is in Sahih Muslim. Our Prophets SAW said, "Whoever drinks from the Hawd, shall never ever be thirsty for all of eternity". Can you imagine, one sip of that Hawd, and that is it. For the rest of eternity, you will never be thirsty.

Can you imagine the power of Hawd? And this is just the first sip of Jannah. What do you think awaits us in Jannah? if this will be the one sip of one Fountain of Jannah, that we shall Inshallah taste on the day of Judgement.

Now question arises here that, well, if we will never get thirsty after this, why would we be drinking from the fountains of Jannah? When Allah SWT says that, there are fountains of milk and there are fountains of honey and their fountains of pure alcohol, in which there is no negatives. All of these fountains are in Jannah.

Why will we drink, when we're not thirsty? The response is that, the food and the drink of Jannah is not meant for us to survive. We don't need food and drink to survive in Jannah. The food and the drink of Jannah is just for pleasure.

For Example, sometimes we are not that hungry, but if a nice dish is presented to you, you'd Just want to taste the dish. So, Jannah will be all of this. In Jannah, you can eat and eat and eat, and you will never get fat. You don't have to worry about your weight. You can eat and eat, and there is no issue of worrying about hunger or getting full.

Because you're not eating for your digestion. It is not the food, that is for your survival. it is just for the pleasure of eating itself. So, whoever tastes from the Hawd, will never ever be thirsty for all of eternity.

Invited to The Hawd

Also, of the things that we learn about the Hawd is that, our Prophet SAW is in charge of the Hawd. Which means he is the one who must invite you. If you are not invited by him, you will not get to the Hawd. He is waiting for us there. He will be there before any of us come.

So, he will be there preparing the Hawd. Then, when he sees batches of people, he shall invite them. And he shall come to his Ummah, calling out to his Ummah.

Hadith of Asma Bin Abu Bakr RA that, she says, "I heard the Prophet SAW saying "I shall be at the Hawd waiting, and I will see who will be coming to present himself in front of me".

So, the Prophet SAW will be the one who will be waiting and he is going to be seeing who is coming to him, and inviting people to the Hawd. And he shall be recognizing people from the Wudu. The Prophet SAW will see them from the entire mankind and invite them to come to the Hawd.

Special Status at The Hawd

People will come in batches, depending on their faith. So, the stronger Iman, or those that were more blessed, will be coming to the Hawd earlier. And there will be special people as well on that day, that gets special privilege; because of who they are, and because of what they've done.

This is mentioned in a number of traditions. Of them, is the Hadith of Tawban RA. He says that the prophet SAW said, "My fountain is going to be from Aden to Amman. Its water is whiter than milk. It is sweeter than honey. The number of cups is more than the stars in the sky. Whoever drinks from it, shall never be thirsty".

And then, he SAW says, "The first batch, who shall come to the fountain, will be the poor of the Muhajireen". The number one batch that will come to the Hawd, will be those who left everything in Makkah and migrated to Medina.

He SAW described them, "Their hairs were disheveled. Their clothes were dusty. They were not able to marry women that were upper class. They were people whose doors would not open for them. They will be the first batch to drink from the Hawd".

So, because they didn't have the money, they weren't able to get nice partners in the social economic sense.

Obviously, Iman and Taqwa is separate. The Prophet SAW is describing the poor of the Muhajireen.

One Sahaba narrated this Hadith after the death of the Prophet SAW, and Umar RA happened to be sitting there, and he began to cry. And he said, "As for me, then I am not fitting this category. Because I have been able to marry ladies of a rich social economic status. I have good clothing. And my hair is not to disheveled and dusty. Perhaps I should wear simple clothing and allow my hair to become disheveled and dusty".

Umar RA felt that he is not going to meet this criterion. But of course, this is Umar RA. He is one of the ten who were promised Jannah in this world. But this shows his Iman and Taqwa, that he felt this way. Because he is of this rank as well.

How about the Ansar? There is a beautiful hadith in the Musnad of Imam Ahmed, that mentions that even the Ansar will be of the earliest of the batches. This hadith goes as follows that, Hamza RA, when he migrated to Medina, he married one of the ladies from the Ansar.

The Prophet SAW, He would regularly visit Hamza RA. So, this hadith is about the first two years of Medina. Because Hamza RA died a shaheed in the Battle of Uhud. So, he is visiting the House of Hamza RA regularly and he would mention to them Hadith.

One day he came to the House of Hamza RA, and his wife said that, "O Messenger of Allah SWT, I have heard the people say that you will have a fountain on the day of Judgement, that is very massive and large".

The Prophet SAW said, "Yes, and the most beloved people to me that will come to that fountain to drink, will be your people, that is the Ansar".

In another Hadith, in Musnad of Imam Ahmed, He SAW also said that, "I will be at the Hawd clearing the way for the people of Yemen. So that they will be given a spot in the Hawd". So, the people of Yemen are praised so much in this Hadith.

May be, it is because they are undergoing a severe catastrophe, and the sad reality is that it is a manmade catastrophe. The even sadder reality is that it is being caused by our Muslim brethren.

The point being that according to this hadith, the Prophet SAW will see the people of Yemen coming, and he's going to clear the way for them. What a beautiful blessing it is for the people of Yemen that the Prophet SAW himself is going to make sure that they have a special spot, so that they can drink from the Hawd. So, this shows us that There will be people that have special status at the Hawd.

Prevented from The Hawd

We also have one of the characteristics of the Hawd, which is also one of the scariest ones. It is mentioned in over 10 hadith about this. That there will be people whom the Prophet SAW will recognize and he will call out to them. But then the Angels will come and prevent them from getting to the Hawd.

There are many hadith about this. There is a Hadith of Ume Salama RA, where she says that, "I used to hear the people mentioning the fountain and I had not heard the Prophet SAW directly mentioned the fountain. And one day, my little girl servant was combing my hair and I heard the Prophet SAW say, 'All people, come'. So, I said to my servant little girl that I'm going to go out".

She said that, "He SAW is calling the men and not the women". Ume Salama RA said, "No. He SAW said 'O people', and I am from the people". She rushed to the Masjid, and there she heard the Prophet SAW say that, "I will be the one that is waiting for you at the fountain. But Be careful, let nobody come to you on that day, that is going to be turned back away from me. Be careful from being amongst that group".

The Prophet SAW continued, "I will say, why are they being turned away from me?" And the Prophet SAW said that he will be told, "You do not know how they changed after you". Then Prophet SAW said, "I will say be gone, be gone".

This hadith is in Tirmidhi, but the concept of group of people being turned away, it is in Bukhari, and Muslim, and in every book of hadith. That the prophet SAW will call out and He will say that these are his people. These are his companions from his group. But the Angels will say, "You do not know how they changed. You do not know what they introduced. You do not know that they turned their backs and they left".

This hadeeth is a very deep and profound hadith. Ibn Hajar RA and Imam An-Nawawi RA and so many of the classical Ulema, they have discussed this, this group could be that of the hypocrites. It could also be those who followed the false prophets. There are people who followed false prophets, and the civil wars that took place and their false prophets were on the other side.

It could also be people who committed major sins. Because these people are not non-Muslims. These people are Muslims, but the Prophet SAW is saying, "You're not going to have the blessing of drinking from my fountain". They might still end up in Jannah. But there is a blessing on the day of Judgement, and that blessing shall be to drink from the fountain.

So, it is possible there will be groups of people who have committed major sins and that is something that is very realistic. Therefore, we need to try our best to follow the Sunnah, by respecting the Sunnah and to be of those whom the Prophet SAW invites and nobody comes in between.

Incentive for Being Patient

Also, an interesting point about the Hawd is that, in multiple narrations, our prophet SAW, He mentioned the Hawd as an incentive for the companions to remain steadfast, to make them go through difficult times.

Of them, for example, we already mentioned this Hadith in previous chapter that, after the Prophet SAW prayed over the people of Uhud, meaning, after the incident of Uhud took place, he went to the Mosque, and he climbed the Minbar, as if to bid farewell.

According to one report, this is one of the last sermons that he SAW ever gave in his life. In fact, this might be the last general Khutbah he ever gave to all of his Sabah in the Masjid of the Prophet SAW.

Realize, right before the Prophet SAW passed away, he visited Uhud one last time, and then he came back, and then he gave a sermon. For many of the Sabah, this was the last time they saw him.

Do you know what he said? How he began that sermon? He said, "I shall meet you at the Hawd". So, may be, Allah SWT knows best, he SAW knew that this is the last time the Sahabah are going to see him. Hence, he is reminding them that, "Don't worry, wait for me at the Hawd, and I'll be there for you at the Hawd".

Also, in another Hadith reported in Abu Dawood and others, where he was speaking to the Ansar. He said to them that, "You're going to face many disasters and calamities after me. So, be patient until you meet me at the fountain".

So, what an amazing Hadith. Imagine now what is he talking about. The companions, they faced a lot of trials and tribulations in their lifetimes. There was a lot of negative things that went on in that time frame. The massacre of Uthman RA, the assassination of Umar RA and Ali RA, the attempted assassination of so many other Sahabah, the civil wars between the Sahabah etc.

The early antics of the Umayyad dynasty, and the event of Karbala; all of these things that happened. Very negative tragedies. Very sad tragedies. Our Prophet SAW is telling the Ansar, "You're going to see some difficult things ahead of you. So be patient. Be patient, and I'll be waiting for you at the Hawd".

Imagine the psychology of these Hadiths. They are being told that they should have an incentive of being reunited with the Prophet SAW, and to be patient in this world. That it is only a matter of time before the day of judgement happens, and they'll see the Prophet SAW over there.

So, the Hawd and the fountain is being used as an incentive for the Sahaba to be righteous and to maintain a level head through times of trial and tribulation. The same applies for us as well.

Chronology of The Hawd

Now, when will the Hawd take place? It is not clear if the Hawd will take place necessarily after or before the Mizan and Scrolls and Hisab. In reality we're not 100% certain, if it will it be before the Hisab, or will it be after the Hisab? Will it be before the Sirat, or will it be after the Sirat right before Jenna?

There's a number of interpretations in this regard. Out of them, the two are main interpretations. The first opinion, is the opinion of Imam Al Bukhari RA, and it is also the position of Imam Al Ghazali RA and Imam As-Suyuti RA, and Al Qa'deyat RA. The first opinion is that, the fountain is going to be right before entering the gates of Jannah, after crossing over the Sirat.

So, you will crossover the Sirat and You will come to this area called the Qantara, and at the Qantara, when you're about to enter Jannah, there's going to be the Hawd. What is the evidence?

The evidence is the famous hadith of Anas Ibn Malik RA, that our Prophet SAW was asked by Anas Ibn Malik RA, "Where shall I meet you on the day of Judgement?" The Prophet SAW said, "The first place you should look for me is at the beginning of the Sirat". Anas RA said, "What if I don't find you there?" He SAW said, "Then at the Mizan". Anas RA again said, "If I don't find you there?" He SAW said, "Then at the Hawd. And you will not find me missing from these three places on the day of Judgement".

Imam As-Suyuti RA, he said that, it is narrated in the Hadith of Musnad Al Hakim that, the Hawd will be after the Sirat. So, we have a whole Galaxy of Ulema, that say that the Hawd is going to be after the Sirat, and after the Hisab, and after Mizan, and right before entering Jannah.

Ibn Hajar RA comments, in his commentary of Sahih Bukhari, and he says, "The fact that Imam Buhari RA places the Hadith of the Hawd after the Hadith of the Sirat, this indicates that Imam Buhari believes that the fountain will be after crossing over the bridge".

That is one opinion. However, The Hadith about Hawd in Musnad Al Hakim is not authentic. Secondly, if you look at the Hadith of Anas Ibn Malik RA, Prophet SAW is not describing the order of events specifically. Our Prophet SAW is simply saying, "I'll be at these three places. The clearest place you'll find me is going to be at the Sirat".

Because the Prophet SAW will be at the beginning of the Sirat. He SAW is going to be waiting for the people at this Sirat. There's only one bridge, and he's at the front of that bridge. So, this is going to be the easiest place to find him. So, this is why the first place the Prophet SAW said to look for him was the Sirat.

Then He said the Mizan and the Hawd. And that he is going to be at these three locations. This hadith is not telling us a chronological order. It simply giving three locations. In all likelihood, what it means is that, statistically speaking, it is easiest to find the Prophet SAW at Sirat, then at Mizan and then at Hawd. Because of the number of people that will decrease as we keep moving forward with each stage of the day of judgment. Perhaps, it has nothing with chronology. Perhaps it has to do with the frequency of people.

The other opinion which is the opinion of Imam Al Qurtubi RA and Ibn Kathir RA and others, that the Hawd is going to be before they Sirat and even before the Mizan. The Hawd is going to be even before the judgement.

Rather it will be as soon as one gets out of the graves. Because, at that time people will be thirsty, and one will be able to drink before the Hisab, before the Mizan, before Allah SWT is speaking one on one with us.

Ibn Kathir RA narrates that, it appears that the Hawd will be before the Sirat, because only the believers will cross the Sirat. So, there's no need to sift the evil people from the believers; As is going to happen at the Hawd.

This is a very interesting point here. Ibn Kathir RA is perceptively saying that the Hadith says that, the Angels are going to come and say, "These people should not drink from the Hawd". This cannot occur before entering heaven. Because once you get to that stage, everybody's going in Jannah. So, it has to occur before Sirat.

Ibn Kathir RA also says that another way to reconcile between the Hadith is that there are multiple Hawd. So, you should know that, a small group of Ulema, they posited multiple fountains. One is going to be before the Sirat, other is going to be after the Sirat. Nonetheless, it doesn't make sense to have multiple fountains.

Imam Al-Qurtubi RA says that, it would make logical sense if the Hawd is before the Sirat, because people will exit from their graves thirsty. So, Hawd should come to them before the Sirat and before the Mizan.

Meaning, according to Imam Al-Qurtubi RA, even before the judgement, even before the Hisab, even before Mizan; as soon as people are resurrected from the grave, and they enter into the plains of Judgement Day, and the Sun will be there, and the heat will be there; it makes sense that the Hawd is right then and there.

Anybody who's righteous, anybody who's been doing Wudu, anybody who follows the Sunnah, and who wants to hear the Prophet SAW and follow him, that person will be able to drink. So that the terror of the day of Judgement and the thirst of the day of Judgement, they will be free of that.

So, from a rational perspective, meaning, when thinking about the purpose of the Hawd, it makes sense that the Hawd is going to be before all of that takes place.

One of the scholars, worked on the Hadiths of the Day of Judgement and he to compile all of the descriptions of the day of Judgement. He has around 100 pages about the Hawd. He then concludes at the very end of it that, "It appears from all of the above that, the fountain will be on the plains of the Day of Judgement. Before the Sirat. Before the Mizan, and before the judgement. Before anything actually happens, there will be the Hawd".

Misconception About Hawd

Now, there is a common perception, or a myth, or a cultural connotation, that Prophet SAW will be giving the Kawthar or the Hawd from his own hands. In other words, the people will be drinking Hawd from hands of Prophet SAW himself.

This phrasing is not found in the Quran or in the Sunnah. We can say metaphorically, he is giving it with his hands, meaning he is inviting the people. But technically, he will not be the one picking up the water and putting it in our mouths. That is not valid.

Our scholars say that this issue of the Prophet SAW, giving from the Hawd with his own hands; not only is it not narrated, it doesn't even make sense. That the Prophet SAW, he is the one to whom the Hawd belongs to, shall become the water feeder.

Rather it is befitting that, he will be inviting people to the Hawd, and not that he will be feeding himself to millions and millions of people. But rather that he is in charge of it. And we should make Dua to Allah SWT that we are of those that are invited and not of those that are rejected.

We want to drink from the Hawd. we wanted the Prophet SAW to invite us and to recognize us. And we want to drink from that pool, whiter than milk itself, sweeter than honey, and that whoever drinks it will never be thirsty after that. So, we pray that Allah SWT blesses us to drink from the Hawd on the day of Judgement, so that we do not have to face any thirst after that.

The Separation of Mankind

Now, according to our knowledge of what we have in the Quran and Sunnah, we're getting to the end of what we know of what's going to happen on the day of judgment. The next stage is of course going to be Jannah. We ask Allah SWT for that. Or it will be Jahannam. We seek Allah SWT's refuge from that.

Now, the beginnings of that winding down are going to take place by gathering people according to the camps that they were in. So, what's going to happen is the demarcation of various groups of people. There will be the segregation or the separation of groups of people.

The believers will be in one group; And all of those who believed in other gods, they would be resurrected in accordance with the gods that they believed in. Meaning, on that day, at this time frame, people will be separated based upon their gods which is based upon their religions.

Therefore, this will demonstrate for us the real separation; and those who worshipped other than Allah SWT, those who rejected the worship of Allah SWT, they will be separated from the believers.

The Quran mentions that, they will then be dragged on their faces to Jahannam. There will come a point in time, where they will be made blind and deaf and dumb. There will come a point in time, where their senses will be operating again. As explained in the chapters before, that there will possibly be variations during that time frame.

Then, they're going to feel Jahannam, sense Jahannam, see Jahannam. They will beg Allah SWT to come back at that stage again. They will also, at that stage as well, regret and wish to go back in this world. So that, they don't have to see all of this punishment.

Each group will be resurrected following its gods and its leaders. Meaning the false gods, and the false leaders. Every single group shall be resurrected based upon the people whom they looked up to, the religions that they followed, and the gods that they worship.

Allah SWT mentions this multiple times in the Quran, and it is mentioned in the sunnah as well. For example, in Surah As-Saffat verse number 22, Allah SWT says, "Gather and resurrect those who did wrong to themselves and their helpers. And gather them with those whom they worshiped besides Allah SWT. And then usher them into Jahannam. And cause them to stop. They will be questioned about what they have done".

Allah SWT mentions in the Quran about the people of Firoun in Surah Hud verse 98, "He shall lead his people on the day of judgment, and their end result is going to be the fire of hell". So, Firoun is going to be the leader of his people. Anybody who looked up to Firoun. Anybody who worshipped Firoun. Anybody who took Firoun as a false god.

Anybody who followed that religion, will be resurrected upon the leaders of that religion, and their false gods will be there as well. Those who worship the sun, those worship the moon, they will see either the actual sun and moon, or a replica of that. Then they're going to be told to go to that area. Those who worship other than Allah SWT will be resurrected according to their false gods.

Hadith of Abu Saeed Al Khudri RA

Now, one of the most important traditions about the day of judgment is the lengthy hadith from Abu Saeed Al Khudri RA, that describes multiple things about the day of judgment. We have discussed bits and portions of it from the beginning and we have left certain things to the end.

So, we will do this entire hadith from the words of our Prophet SAW. This hadith, even though it talks about other things, it spends the most amount of time talking about the division of mankind. It is a hadith reported in Bukhari and Muslim.

In Sahih Muslim, it is hadith number 453. Abu Saeed Al Khudri RA says that a group of people asked the Messenger SAW, "Will we see Allah SWT on the day of judgment?" The Prophet SAW said, "Yes, you shall".

Then the Prophet SAW said that, "Do you have any problem seeing the sun is shining bright in the full midday and there's no clouds?" They said, "Of course not. We see the sun". Then he SAW said, "Do you have a problem seeing the full moon in the middle of the month and there's no cloud?" They said, "No."

Our Prophet SAW then said, "In the same way, you shall have no problems looking at Allah SWT on the day of judgment. Just like you can sense the sun and the moon, everyone will equally see Allah SWT".

Then Prophet SAW said, "When it will be the day of judgment, an entity shall proclaim (most likely an Angel), 'Let every group follow what it chooses to worship'. So, no one shall be left, because everybody worships something".

Even if they rejected Allah SWT, they're worshiping themselves. Even atheists have something they look up to. They have something that they consider sacred. So, everybody shall be divided based upon that which they used to worship.

The Prophet SAW said that, "Those who worship idols and stones besides Allah SWT, they will follow them into Jahannam. None shall be left except those who used to worship Allah SWT".

Meaning, the only people that we will be left are those who worshiped Allah SWT. The righteous and the sinful Muslims. The sinful Muslims shall remain with the righteous Muslims. Because in the end of the day, their God was one. Their religion was one. The lord was one.

So, at this point, they're all going to be together. Also, there's going to be some people of the book as well that are going to be left. Our scholars, some have said that, the people that will be left over here are those that are the correct people.

We believe as Muslims that the people of book were righteous and they worshipped Allah SWT properly. And in their time frames, they were rightly guided. So those of them are separate. The real followers of Jesus, the real followers of Moses; the righteous amongst them, who believed in them, in that appropriate time frames, will be left.

Because again, every Prophet AS comes and cancels the previous Prophet AS. Meaning that he supersedes them. We believe that the righteous Jews in the time of Musa AS are Muslims, and the righteous Christians in the time of Isa AS are Muslims. Therefore, they shall be with the righteous. They shall be in a group with their Prophets AS.

How about those that were not righteous, and they rejected the next Prophet AS? These are people who were not righteous to Allah SWT, not faithful to Allah SWT and rejecting the Prophets AS of Allah SWT. They shall remain, and the Muslims shall remain. But the idolaters have now been taken to Jahannam.

Then the Yahood are going to be asked, "What did you use to worship? They would say, "We worshipped the son of Allah SWT". It will be said to them, "You are lying. Allah SWT does not have a partner or a child". Then they shall then be dragged into a Jahannam.

Then the Christians are going to be asked, "What did you use to worship?" They will say, "We used to worship Al-Masih". It will be said to them, "You are lying. Allah SWT did not have a son nor a partner". Then, they too will be dragged into a punishment.

Then no one will be left except the believers, those who worship Allah SWT. Then hadith says that, "Then their lord shall come to them in a form that is the least recognizable fashion".

Meaning, they will not recognize that this is their lord. Hadith continues, "Then their lord will say, 'What are you waiting for?' And they will respond, 'We are waiting for our lord'. Allah SWT will say, 'I am your lord'. And they will not recognize him. They will say, 'We seek Allah SWT's refuge. We will never worship other than Allah SWT'."

Then, Allah SWT will then ask them, "Is there a sign that you shall recognize, that you shall know that this is your lord?" So, they say, "Yes, there is a sign. There is something that we know, that when we see it, this will be our lord".

Then the Hadith says that, "The shin shall be displayed". The shin is the area of a human being, it is beneath the knee and above the foot. Now, this is the literal meaning. The phrase also has a metaphorical meaning in the Arabic language, which is well known in poetry and in pre-Islamic and early language.

But the Sahabah, by and large, they accepted this to be literal. They say that, Allah SWT will display his Shin. This is also the position of scholars like Ibn Khuzaymah RA, Imam ibn Hanbal RA etc.

Other scholars, including many of our classical scholars understand it to be metaphorical. Including Al-Bayhaqi RA, Al-Baqillani RA, Al-Juwayni RA, Al-Ghazali RA. That the meaning here is that, things will become clear.

This is what the metaphorical meaning is that the matter will become settled. Or the issue is going to reach the level of certainty. Or that the sign will be done. This is how they interpret this phrase of the Hadith. What is that sign? According to the second school, we do not know. According to the first school, the sign is to see the shin of Allah SWT.

Hadith continues, "And when that happens, no one who used to prostrate to Allah SWT in this world of his own accord shall remain standing. When they recognize this to be Allah SWT, everybody shall fall down in sajdah".

Meaning, everyone standing that used to worship Allah SWT upon Iman and Ikhlas, they shall all fall down in sajdah. However, those who used to worship Allah SWT to show off to others, those who used to prostrate out of fear of the people, they will not be able to prostrate.

Their backs will become straight. When they try to prostrate, they will fall flat onto their faces. Or they will fall flat onto their backs. Now, this is the separation of the Munafiq and the hypocrites from the righteous and the sinful.

So, we have three categories in this group of people. In this dunya, that all were called Muslims. In the Akhira, they will be resurrected as one group. Within Muslims, there are three categories. The first are the righteous. The people of Taqwa and Iman. The second are going to be the evil sinners. They're Muslims, but they have committed murder. They have not worshipped Allah SWT properly. But they still say the Kalema. The third is the hypocrite. That is the worst of the three.

So, according to this narration, the Mu'min and the sinner will be able to prostrate to Allah SWT. But the hypocrite will not be able to prostrate to Allah SWT. They will be exposed in front of the people.

Then Hadith Continues, "And when they will raise their heads up again (the Mu'min and the sinner), Allah SWT will now appear to them in the form they first saw him". In other words, when the initial presentation of mankind took place.

Meaning, when they prostrate to Allah SWT, then raise their heads up, they will now recognize Allah SWT, because he shall appear to them in the same fashion or manner that they first saw him at the very beginning of the day of judgement. This is now the separation.

Hadith Continues, "Then the bridge will be placed over Jahannam. And intercession will begin. And the people will say, 'Oh Allah SWT we ask for your safety. Keep us safe. Keep us safe".

The Sahaba said, "Oh Messenger of Allah SWT, what is this bridge?" The Prophet SAW said, "The bridge is something that is not steady and firm. But rather it is like a void that you can slip off of".

So, the Prophet SAW described the bridge with adjectives. He did not describe the essence of the bridge. He described the qualities of the bridge. The void means that which is not firm, and that you're going to slip on it. You can easily slip and fall down. So, neither is it firm, nor can you put your feet on it, as you're going to easily slip.

Then Prophet SAW says, "In it will be hooks and tongs and spits, that are like the thorns of a tree in Nadja, called As- Sa'dan". So Sa'dan is a tree in northern Arabia, that has long spiky thorns. So, the hooks are actually going to have thorns on them.

Then Prophet SAW says, "And then the believers are going to pass by. The first to go, will go like at the speed of lightning. Then some will go like the wind. Then some will go like the bird. Then some will go like the fastest horses. Then some will go like the fastest camels. Then some of them are going to be saved without any scratches and harm. Then there will be those that will have scratches, but they will be let go".

So, the hooks are going to come and scratch them. But they'll still manage to go through and get to the other side.

Prophet SAW said, "And there will be those that will be caught up, and dragged, and pushed into the fire of Jahannam".

So, there's three categories that are going to be crossing the bridge. The first, nothing happens to them. The second, they are scared. But they get to the end. The third are those that don't make it, and they're going to be dragged into the fire of hell.

Then the Prophet SAW said, "By the time then that the believers are now safe from the fire of hell, and they've crossed over; the groups that have crossed over, they know who has not crossed over".

Then the Prophet SAW said a very powerful phrase. The Prophet SAW said, "I swear by the one in whose hands is my life, that there will be none amongst you that will be more eager to claim a right, than the believers on the day of resurrection, for their brethren who have been in the fire of hell".

Meaning, No one will argue more passionately, than the believers in front of Allah SWT, to save their brethren. You've never had a more passionate argument, you've never made a stronger case, you've never pleaded with more certainty, and with more passion, and with more enthusiasm, that is the time of pleading.

When the believers who have passed over and they see some of their brethren that have not passed over; they're going to beg Allah SWT, plead Allah SWT, make Shafa'a to Allah SWT, with regards to those brethren that have not crossed over the bridge.

The Prophet SAW said that, "The believers will say, 'O Allah SWT, those people that didn't make it, they prayed with us, and fasted with us, and they did hajj with us.' So, Allah SWT will say to the believers that have made it over, 'Go ahead and get take out anybody whom you recognize'. And Allah SWT will forbid the fire of hell from touching them. A lot of people will be brought out from Jahannam. And the fire of hell would have gone to the middle of their shin, or to their knees. But it would not have gone to their actual bodies."

Hadith continues, "Then they will say, 'O our lord, no one is left that you have commanded us to take out'. Then Allah SWT will say, 'Go back. Whoever you find, who has one coin's weight of good, take him out'. So, they're going to take out a large group of people. Then they will say that, 'O Allah SWT anybody you've told us to with that condition, we have taken him out'."

Then Allah SWT will say, "Go back, and whoever you find that has half a coin's weight Iman, take him out". So, they will take out a large group of people, and they will say, "O Allah SWT, no one whom you commanded for us to take out is left".

Then Allah SWT will say, "Go back, and if you find anybody who has a mustard seed weight (meaning smallest amount or atom's weight) of Iman, take him out". So, they will take out a large group, and they will say, "O Allah SWT, we have left no one according to your conditions".

Here Abu Saeed Al Khudri RA paused the hadith, and he said, "if you don't believe me, then read the Quran". The Ayah quoted in Hadith is, "Allah SWT does not wrong anyone, and whoever has an atom's weight of a good deed, Allah SWT will exaggerate that and give it more. And he will give a great reward because of that".

Then Abu Saeed Al Khudri RA goes back to the hadith. Then Allah SWT will say, "The Angels have interceded, and the Prophets AS have interceded, and the believers have interceded. The only one who is left is Allah SWT, the most merciful of all who have mercy".

Hadith says, "Then Allah SWT will take out a handful of people who have never done any good". And the handful of Allah SWT cannot be compared with anything that we know. But it will be a large amount. More than we can imagine.

Now, this group of people, the other believers did not even recognize them. They have not done any good worthy of mention. Yet, Allah SWT knows that they have something that is worthwhile that is in them. So, they shall be taken out by the mercy of Allah SWT.

Hadith says, "They have been burnt to a crisp. They have been burnt into complete charcoal. These people will be thrown into a river in heaven, that is called the river of life. They shall sprout from this river, the way that a seed sprouts forth that has been carried from the silt of a flood".

It's a very interesting metaphor that the Prophet SAW is giving. That imagine a seed is lying in the dust and people ignore it. Then the rain falls, and the rain comes, and it carries these seeds to a fertile soil and then it plants it somewhere.

Our Prophet SAW said, "Don't you see that, if the seed comes close the stone, or near the tree, that if it is facing the sun, it's going to be slightly yellow or slightly green. And if it is under the shade, then it will be slightly white".

So, he's very specifically saying that, these seeds they will have different colors depending on where they are planted. The Sahaba said, "O Messenger of Allah SAW, it is as if to tend flocks in the desert".

Then the Prophet SAW said, "They shall be taken out like pearls. And they shall have seals around their necks. And the people of Jannah will know and recognize these people. The people of Jannah will say, 'These are the ones whom Allah SWT freed'. And they will entered into Jannah without any good that they have done".

Allah SWT chose them to be in Jannah and they didn't earn anything of Jannah. Allah SWT freed them from his pure mercy. "They are called the Utaka of Allah SWT". Utaka means the one who has been freed by the compassionate one.

Then, "Allah SWT will tell these people that, 'Go ahead and enter Jannah, and whatever you find in there it is for you'. So, they will thank Allah SWT and say, 'O Allah SWT, you have given us that which you have not given any other person'."

Meaning that to be entered into Jannah without any good deeds. This is a blessing that Allah SWT is going to give a group of people. They're going to be the last batch to enter Jannah. No batch enters Jannah after them.

Then, "Allah SWT will say, 'I have something even more precious than this'. They will say, 'What is more precious than what you have given us? You saved us from Jahannam. We're in Jannah. Now, we have everything we can see around us.' Allah SWT will say, 'My pleasure. From now on, I shall never be angry for all of eternity'."

Now, this is a beautiful very long hadith. And it is one of the fundamental hadith of this chapter. We should be aware of it and remember it.

Separated by faith

Now I want to extract from this hadith a number of benefits. Of the benefits that we extract from this very beautiful hadith is that, the real division amongst mankind is not based upon skin color, or the place of birth, or heritage, or passport, or ethnicity, or language, or where you live.

The real division is based upon the religion. It is based upon the god that you worship. That's something you choose. Where you're born, and your skin color, and your heritage, you cannot choose that. And to divide people based upon that is utterly superficial. It is paganistic.

Why would you discriminate against somebody based upon something that is not in his control? Isn't that shallow? But the Sharia does not do that. That's why in terms of race, and in terms of culture, and in terms of heritage, and in terms of skin color, all of humanity is equal.

Allah SWT doesn't care what the color of your passport, or the color of your skin is. How you are divided on the day of judgment, it's not going to be based upon nation or state. All those of you who are so obsessed with your heritage, with your skin color, with your nation and state, overcome this superficiality. It is the essence of paganism.

Concentrate more on your primary identity. Your primary identity through which you shall be recognized, and you shall be separated, is the identity of your faith. What you believe, what you consider sacred, the god that you worship, that is what defines you. So, be careful that you don't take these superficial things and make them primary.

There's nothing wrong with recognizing your heritage, and your passport, and your skin color, as long as you're not looking down at other people. We all have our heritages. But it is definitely wrong to make those the end all and the be all. Anybody who does so, you have taken those things as your primary demarcation. And on the day of judgment, that's not the primary demarcation.

Whom He Loves and Worships

Also, we learn here that, our Prophet SAW said, "A person shall be with those whom he loves and worships". So, if you loved Allah SWT, you will be resurrected with those who worshipped Allah SWT. If you love the believers, if you identify with the believers, you will be resurrected with the believers.

Better Than the Idolaters

Of the benefits as well, that we see over here is that, even the rejecters from the people of the book are better than the idolaters, and from the Mushrikeen. This is demonstrated by the fact that they remain when everybody else goes to Jahannam. Then of course, because they rejected Allah WT, so then they too are going to go to Jahannam.

But in this world, and in the Akhira, certain perks and privileges are given to them. Even those that rejected the other Prophets AS. Obviously, the Ahel Al kitab that were righteous and believed in their Prophets AS at the right time frame, they are Muslims.

We're talking about the Ahel Al kitab who were not loyal to Allah SWT. They are still better than the ones who worshipped statues and stones. Because the worship of Allah SWT through the religions of the Ahel Al kitab is still infinitely more logical and rational than the worship of a stone that you carve, or an idol that you yourself have created.

Companionship of the Believers

Also, another benefit that we get from this hadith is that, the wicked of the believers and the hypocrites of the believers, just like they enjoyed the physical companionship of the believers, and the perks of the Ummah, so too they will enjoy it for a period of time on the day of judgment..

By the end of the day of judgment, they will all be together. But then separations are going to occur. How will those separations occur?

The hypocrites they will not even get to the Sirat. Because they're not going to even be able to get there. The sinful of the believers, they shall get to the Sirat, and some amongst them are going to fall into Jahannam

Final Test on the Day of judgment

We also learn from this as well that, there is going to be a final test on the day of judgment, and that test is that, the believers are going to be left for a period of time in suspense of not knowing what is going on. They don't know what is going on.

After all of the other false religions, they have been taken into Jahannam, led by their false gods, and no one will be left on the planes of the day of judgment other than the believers; the panic will rise amongst the mainstream groups of people and the mainstream believers, the average muslim.

They're going to be wondering, what's going on. Then they will see an entity and not recognize that entity to be Allah SWT. When the entity says, "I am your lord.", they will seek refuge and they will say, "No we never did Shirk in this world. We're not going to do shirk now".

Subhan Allah, this is one final test that when they don't recognize Allah SWT, and they think that this entity is not Allah SWT, they say we cannot worship this. We were firm in this dunya. We will not turn back in the Akhirah.

This shows us that those who are committed to Iman and Taqwa, and those that are firm in this dunya, Allah SWT will bless them in the Akhirah as well.

Now we also have to mention here that, indeed the average muslim might be worried, or concerned, or in suspense. However not from this hadith, but from generic texts in the Quran, we learn that the righteous amongst the believers are not going to be in any panic or suspense.

We learn that the righteous, Muslims of the highest category, and the people of Ihsan, Allah SWT says in the Quran, "They're never going to worry. They're never going to grieve".

Allah SWT says in the Quran, "Those who won the race, those who are at the very forefront, Allah SWT will promise them Jannah. They're not even going to hear Jahannam. They're not even going to be worried on the day of the great worry".

So, amongst this category, there will be those that have absolutely no worry whatsoever. Now what is the wisdom of this final test that Allah SWT is coming, and Allah SWT is saying, "I am your lord". And the believers are not going to recognize Allah SWT.

The wisdom, and Allah SWT knows best, is that, this is the stage where the hypocrites will be separated from the pious, and the hypocrites will not be able to prostrate fully to Allah SWT. So, this is the wisdom here that, those who passed this test were not hypocrites. Then the hypocrites will now be taken away, and dragged to Jahannam.

Then only the believers are left, that had some sincerity, or more sincerity, or the most sincerity. Meaning, anybody who was a genuine muslim, and had genuine Iman. Even if, they were sinful, they were murderers, they were taking drugs, or doing Zina.

All of that might be there. They're not righteous Muslims. They're not worshiping Allah SWT properly. They're breaking their trust. But deep down inside, they believe in Allah SWT and his Messenger SAW. That Kalema is more precious than any other deed ever. So, anybody who said the Kalema with an ounce of Iman and Taqwa, they will remain over there.

Of course, once Allah SWT then comes to them, and gives them the sign, then anybody who did sajdah from his own accord, will not remain standing. But rather be in sajdah.

Shafa'a on Sirat

Another point to benefit in these narrations is that, our Prophet SAW said, "The bridge is going to be placed over Jahannam, and then the Shafa'a will be allowed". Now this is a very clear indication that, the Shafa'a of the believers will take place at this stage.

As for the Shafa'a of the Prophets AS, we already mentioned in the chapter about Shafa'a in a lot of detail, that the Shafa'a of the Prophets AS is in multiple levels. It will take place at different time frames. So, the Shafa'a of the Prophets AS, some categories have already come and some categories are going to come along with the believers.

But the rest of the believers, the Shafa'a begins after the bridge is set up and they cross over. That is when their shaft begins. This is befitting because, only when the believer has known that he himself is being saved, then he can argue on behalf of somebody else.

Some scholars have said that, this is one type of Shafa'a and the believers might have another type of Shafa'a before this time frame. And Allah SWT knows best. All of this is something that we really do not know for sure.

Two Helpers on Sirat

Another thing that is very interesting in one version of this hadith is that, the Prophet SAW said, "Two things will stand next to the bridge as people pass by, encouraging and affirming those people. Two things will act as helpers for those that cross the bridge. The two things are trust and family".

Because we want to cross the bridge with certainty, and we want to cross the bridge with firmness. Therefore, those two things are, trust and family. Were you a trustworthy person? Did you fulfill your promises? Did you act in an ethical manner in whatever you did? Well if you did, then trust will come and support you as you cross the bridge.

How are you with your family? How are you with your parents, your siblings, and your children? How were you with your extended family? Were you a loving father, or son, or daughter, or brother? Were you a person who fulfilled the ties of kinship? Were you one who went out of your way to make sure your family was taken care of?

Were you able to take care of them? Or were you one who cut off the ties of kinship? If you were a good family member, then the concept of family itself will support you as you cross the bridge.

Shafa'a of Prophet SAW

Another point of benefit we gain from this is that, the Prophets AS themselves are worried about their ummah. We learn in the hadith that the Prophet SAW himself is going to be standing at the end, at the other side of the Sirat. Or according to some scholars, he SAW will be standing at the beginning, before you cross over the Sirat.

And the Prophet AS are going to be saying that, "Grant peace, O Allah. Grant peace to those that are crossing over". This indicates the love that all Prophets AS had.

Especially our Prophet Muhammad SAW, at every stage of the day of judgment, when he is giving water with the Hawd, when the Mizan is being placed; at the very beginning he's making Shafa'a, and at the very end, he is making Shafa'a.

So, from the beginning to the end, our Nabi SAW is concerned about his ummah. He's concerned about all of us. Therefore, there is no question that, some people will be saved from Jahannam at this very end, by the Shafa'a of the Prophet SAW.

Benefit for Believers

Now, notice here that the sinful of the believers, they get to the Sirat, and they start crossing the Sirat, and they then fall from the Sirat into Jahannam. They do not enter Jahannam from the doors of Jahannam.

This indicates that the area that the believers who are sinful are going to be punished, in is a different area, than the main areas of Jahannam.

The believers are not going to occupy the same areas that those who rejected Allah SWT will occupy. The believers will not be dragged into Jahannam the way that those who rejected Allah SWT will be.

The believers will not be made deaf, dumb, and blind. The believers will not even be punished in the same manner as those who rejected Allah SWT and his Messenger SAW.

Those who believe and those who reject Allah SWT are not the same. Even if they commit sins, versus those who reject the Kalema.

Point over here is that, the infinite justice of Allah SWT is demonstrated over here as well. That the believers are going to benefit from safety and security to the very end. Then if they're not worthy of crossing over, then they're going to be taken into Jahannam by the hooks coming in and making them fall into Jahannam.

Therefore, the Quran mentions that, "Those who enter Jahannam from the doors of Jahannam, they will never exit Jahannam". Notice this technicality. Those to enter through the doors of Jahannam will remain therein forever.

Hence, the groups of people in this hadith, that Allah SWT will save, they will not enter Jahannam through the gates of Jahannam. The gates of Jahannam are reserved for the worst of the worst. As for the sinful of the believers, they will neither enter Jahannam through the doors of Jahannam; nor will they enter the same place of Jahannam that the rejecters are occupying.

Those Who Fell Down

Rather, as the Prophet SAW said, "On both sides of the Sirat, there will be hooks that are going to be taken taking those whom Allah SWT command them to take".

Notice the infinite justice of Allah SWT, that even the speed of crossing and the manner of crossing, will be dependent on piety. And it's interesting that hadith follows the physics. That the Prophet SAW said in the hadith, "The first will go as fast as lightning".

So, he made the speed of light the fastest. Then he said, the speed of the wind, and the galloping horse, and the bird etc. But it's just interesting that, when he wanted to set the bar as the highest speed, he said, they shall cross at the speed of light. Which is true. Lightning is the fastest speed according to science. But it was not a known concept at that time.

Now, obviously the faster you're zooming, the less chance the hooks have to catch you. When you're going superfast, the hooks are not going to catch you. Then gradually people are going to become slower, and slower, and slower. Until there will be those that are just dragging, and crawling.

All of this will be proportional to their good deeds and their Iman. So be careful dear Muslims. Your piety and your good deeds will help you in this world all the way until the next and in Jannah. Iman and Taqwa will always benefit you.

You want to cross the Sirat at lightning speed? Make sure you have the light of this dunya, the light of Hidayat, the light of the Quran, and the light of Zikar.

Now, the people are going to be crossing at various speeds. Then some people are going to be scratched. And this in this is the final aspect of punishment. These will be those who deserved a little bit of punishment, but were still good enough to go to Jannah.

The scratches from the hooks are going to be their punishment. It could be because of their backbiting, or their betrayal, or their hurting other people, or they did something that they deserve that last bit of punishment. Because Allah's justice is infinite. But we don't want to be scratched by the thorns of Jahannam.

Then there will be those that the hooks come, and grabs them, and literally drags them down. That is definitely not the category we want to be in.

Now, this hadith does not indicate that all of the Shafa'a will take place right then and there. Rather that the door of Shafa'a will open and will continue for as long as Allah SWT wills. So, the people might even enter Jannah, and after some time, they will think of somebody, whenever Allah SWT wills. Then they will make Shafa'a for them later on.

Hadith does not necessarily indicate that before they get to Jannah everybody is saved. Because that doesn't make sense. People are going to be punished for different time frames in Jahannam. Rather what this indicates is that the doors of Shafa'a by Muslims will open up after the bridge is laid out.

After this point in time, for however long Allah SWT wants, people will continue to remember their relatives, their friends, their business partners, their colleagues, their acquaintances. They'll think of somebody whenever Allah wants them to think of them. Then when they think of that person, they will make Shafa'a for that person to Allah SWT.

Now, the people of the first category are going to be the ones that moved the fastest, and also, they will not be scarred. The Prophet SAW said, "Allah SWT will make the fire of hell haram upon their bodies". And some of those that do fall down, the fire of hell will be to their shin or to their knees. So, they'll feel the heat, but the hell fire is not actually burning them.

Subhan Allah! Subhan Allah! we don't want that. But compared to what's going to happen to the ones that become charcoal, obviously that's better. Who are these people? The believers who prayed, fasted, did hajj.

If you fulfill the five pillars of Islam, even if you have major sins, you shall eventually be interceded for and enter Jannah. And the fire of hell itself shall not actually burn you. But the heat of hell shall be inflicted upon the sinners of that category. And we seek Allah SWT's refuge from that.

There will be some people, who fulfill the five pillars of Islam, but their sins are so much, they will go through Jahannam, but not into Jahannam. They will be punished externally internally.

The fire is going to their ankles, or their shins, or even to their knees. But the fire itself is not going to burn them. This is explicit in the hadith. That's the first category. Everybody who was of this category shall be removed eventually.

Then Allah SWT will allow another category. This is after every person who even has an atom's weight of Iman is allowed to go to Jannah. Then Allah SWT will choose this category of people that never did a good deed of significance. This shows us that we should never lose hope in Allah SWT's mercy.

Allah SWT will say, "I know they deserve to have mercy". So, Allah SWT will take out the last batch. Now, this indicates that the batches before this have not been harmed to this level. That Jahannam and the fire of Jahannam has burnt them to a level of crisp. This batch has been left to the very end of the batches are going to be removed.

This batch is going to be called that the people whom Allah SWT has freed. Now because they've been burned to charcoal, they will be taken into a beautiful river, and they'll be thrown into that river, and then they will come out of the river absolutely fresh and clean.

They shall have a badge of distinction, and the believers in Jannah will recognize them. At that stage there is no animosity, or anger, or looking down. At that stage, everybody is pure-hearted.

They're going to say, "Welcome, you people whom Allah SWT has freed. No one has had that honor that you were given". It is an honor. As they were given Jannah for no good deed of their own. That is something that Allah SWT blessed them with.

The Bridge of Sirat

Now, Sirat is going to be the finale event of the day of judgement. It is the final step right before entering of the gates of Jannah. It is in fact one of the most interesting and also one of the most discussed of these stages of the Day of Judgement.

Out of all of the aspects of the day of Judgement, this one has a special status, because it has become a point of the books of theology. Almost every single classical book that has been written about Islamic theology, it mentions that of the beliefs of Islam, is to believe in the Sirat.

The term Sirat is used in the Quran for multiple meanings. Primarily it is used for the Sirat Al Mustaqim, or the straight path. That's something that is understood. We're not talking about that Sirat. We're talking about another Sirat.

This Sirat is an actual bridge, that will be over Jahannam. It will be connecting the people that are on the actual site and planes of day of judgment to the gates of Jannah. Now, we do not know where the plains of the day of judgement are going to be.

Darkness Before the Bridge

There's a Hadith of Aisha RA. This Hadith is narrated in Sahih Bukhari that, somebody asked the Prophet SAW that, "O Messenger of Allah SWT, the Quran says that on the day of Judgement this earth is going to be substituted for another earth. Where will mankind be on that day, when this earth is going to be gone?"

Our Prophet SAW said, "They are going to be in a darkness that is right before the bridge". He called it Jisr in Hadith, and it as a more specific term for a bridge. Sirat and Jisr are both synonymous for an actual bridge that will be suspended over Jahannam. On one side of the bridge is the planes of the Day of Judgement and on the other side is the gates of Jannah. The only way to get to the gates of Jannah is going to be over the bridge.

Now, this hadith tells us that there's something called a darkness, or a stage of darkness, and this is a very important phase of the day of Judgement. It is one of very important stages that will occur. This stage is actually explicitly mentioned in the Quran, not once, but twice. Two times, the Quran explicitly mentions this stage of darkness.

Allah STW says in Surah Hadid verse 12 to 15 that, "On that day, you shall see the believing men and women. Light will be shining from in front of them, and from the right sides, and they should be given glad tidings of heaven, under which rivers are flowing. Indeed, that is the biggest victory on that day. The hypocrites are going to call out to the believers, and the hypocrites are going to, say, 'Allow us to take guidance from your light'."

So, the hypocrites will not be given light. They're going to see the light of the believers, and they're going to ask them permission for following their light to go to Jannah.

So, Allah STW says in the Quran, "It will be said to them, 'Get away from here. Go find your own light'. And there shall be a large barrier between them and the believers. And on one side of the barrier is going to be mercy. And on the other side is going to be a punishment from Allah SWT".

This verse tells us that, there will be a time frame where there will be no light other than the light coming from the bodies of the believers. And this is going to be right before the Sirat. We learn from this that, towards the end of Judgement Day, all of the people who claimed the name of Islam in this world, and anybody who labeled themselves as Muslims, is going to be in that group.

That group is consisting of people who will go to Jannah directly. And it is consisting of people who will go through Jahannam to Jannah. And it is going to consist of Munafiqun who will not even get close to Jannah.

They were not believers. They didn't have a shred of Iman.

Hypocrites are going to be separated at this stage. How will they be separated? On that day, Allah STW is saying, "The believers are not going to be humiliated by Allah SWT by being taken to Jahannam. And you will find light coming from them. In front of them. And on the right-hand side (Meaning positive light, a blessed light). Then, they're going to say, 'O Allah STW, perfect our light and forgive us. You are capable of all things.'"

Light for The Believers

Our Prophet SAW explained this stage in a Hadith in Sahih Muslim. It is Reported by Jabir Ibn Abdullah. Our Prophet SAW said, "Everybody at that stage, the Mumin and the Munafiq, is going to be given some type of light. Then they're going to follow each other onto the bridge. And on the bridge, there is going to be hooks and there's going to be thorns. And whomever Allah STW wishes, will be dragged in Jahannam through those thorns. Then the light of the Munafiqun will be extinguished. And the light of the believers will save the believers".

So, there will be in darkness right before the bridge. People will need light to find the bridge, and to crossover the bridge, and to guide them into Jannah. That light, where will it come from? Allah SWT will bless Iman to become light for Muslims.

Prophet SAW said, and Hadith is Musnad of Imam Hakim, "They shall be given light. Each one in accordance with their good deeds. Some of them, their light will be like a massive mountain in front of them. Some of them, their light will be even more than a mountain. Some of them, their light will be like a good palm tree. And some of them will be given lesser than this. Until finally the person that is given the lowest light will be to his toe. The toe is going to light up and then go out. Then light up and go out. And every time the toe lights up, he's going to take one step forward. Then that toe becomes dark, and he's going to stay there, not knowing whether the lights going to come back or not".

So, this hadith tells us another thing, that light is going to be given to the believers in accordance with their Iman and their Taqwa and their good deeds. And all of this is a manifestation of Allah SWT's protection and mercy. As you protected the commandments of Allah SWT, and as you showed your piety in this world, so to you shall be protected in the next World in proportionality.

Is it not fair dear Muslims, that the righteous are rewarded? Is it not fair that the ones who went through pain and suffering and were patient, shall be given a manifestation of that blessing? And therefore, according to one's Iman and Taqwa, they shall be rewarded throughout the day of Judgement, and then in Jannah itself.

Of the rewards is that, the more was a person's Iman and the better was a person's deeds, the kinder, the more rituals, the more charity, the more light is going to be.

The actions that increase the light, of them is to sit after the Salah and do Zikr. Of them is to walk to the prayers. Or to drive, in our case. Especially Fajr prayer and Isha prayer. Praying Fajr and Isha in the Masjid is one of the ways to perfect our light on the day of Judgement. There are other things that are given as well by our scholars. Charity and other things are mentioned in some of the books, about how we can increase our light.

As that light will then guide us to the Sirat and then over the Sirat. We seek Allah SWT's refuge, from the hypocrites, as they will not be given a light. Light will be taken away from them. Therefore, they cannot find the bridge and they will then be thrown into Jahannam.

Sirat in Quran

Now we get to the issue of the bridge. The Sirat, is it mentioned in the Quran or not? The majority of scholars say that the Sirat is mentioned in the Quran. However, it is mentioned implicitly, not explicitly. The phrase or the word Sirat does not occur with the bridge. The word Sirat occurs for Sirat Al Mustaqim. But not the Sirat that is over Jahannam.

The implicit reference is in Surah Maryam verse 71. "Everyone amongst you shall arrive to it". Now, what does it means? Our scholars of the past, especially from the time of the Sahabah, there were two opinions.

One position was that, it means to go through. There were some of the Sahabah who said, "Every single human shall go through Jahannam. Some of them will be affected. Some will go through it, without being affected".

However, the majority interpretation and the interpretation that then became the standard, and pretty much everybody in our times believes it, this is now the standard interpretation that, "Everyone amongst you shall cross over Jahannam". Not go through it.

So, it here does not mean to go through Jahannam. It here means to go over Jahannam. So, the Quran mentions that, "Every single one amongst you, without exception, is going to go over Jahannam".

Everybody, including the believers are going to go over Jahannam. As for the hypocrites, and as for the Kafir, they will enter Jahannam. But even the believer shall go over Jahannam.

Sirat in Hadith

The concept of the Sirat is very explicitly mentioned in numerous Hadiths. Of the Hadith that mentions the Sirat, we've already mentioned in previous chapters. Anas Ibn Malik RA said, "O Messenger of Allah SWT, where should I find you on the day of Judgement?" The Prophet SAW said, "First find me at the Sirat". Then, He said, at the Mizan and at the Hawd.

How beautiful it is that Our Prophet SAW, throughout the entire day of judgement, is going to be concerned with his Ummah. Either feeding them water and making sure they are taking care of on the day of Judgement. Or making Shafa'a for them at the Mizan. That the Mizan should be heavy for every Muslim. Or making dua for them to crossover the Sirat and enter Jannah.

His entire day of judgement, Subhan Allah, is going to be for his Ummah. It is not going to be for himself. That's exactly what Allah STW says in the Quran that, "A Messenger has come to you. He is more concerned about you, than he is about himself."

Also, in Hadith of Abu Saeed Al Khudri RA, which we mentioned in the last chapter, the long hadith; The Prophet SAW said that, "Then the bridge will be placed over Jahannam, and I shall be the first one to cross it. And the Prophets AS, all of them will be saying, 'Peace, O Allah SWT, Peace'. And there shall be thorns like the bushes of Sa'dan. They're going to be a size that only Allah SWT knows. And people will be snatched, each one in accordance with their deeds".

In another Hadith in Sahih Muslim, he said, "There are going to be curved hooks that are coming out of Jahannam and dragging people down. These are the Munafiqun". It is also possible that some of the people taken will be from the Sirat will be from the sinful believers. And they're going to be going temporarily into Jahannam as well.

As for the Munafiqun, those hooks will drag them to the lowest parts of Jahannam. Because Allah STW says in the Quran, "The hypocrites will be in the lowest, lowest, lowest parts of Jahannam. And they have a separate punishment for them".

But the sinful of the Muslims, they shall not be dragged into the depths of Jahannam. They shall be in the peripheries of Jahannam. For however long Allah SWT wants them to be. Then, as we explained in our last chapter, they should then be taken out from that area.

Our Prophet SAW said in one hadith that, "Amana and Rahim will stand on each side of the Sirat". Amana means integrity. Amana means speaking the truth. Amana means fulfilling the covenants. Amana means being true to your word. Amana means your Akhlaq as well. And Rahim means the family. Which is how you deal with your family, your spouse, your children, your parents, your extended family. The two main things that will help you cross over the Sirat are your Amana and Rahim.

Then our Prophet SAW said, "And then people will crossover at different speeds. The first of them shall cross like lightning. Then he said the second would be like the twinkling of an eye. Then like a fast bird. Then like a horse. Then like a very quick runner, a jogger. Until the last one is going to be crawling very slowly".

We learn from this as well that, there will be batches going over the Sirat. The first to cross the Sirat are going to be the most righteous of the people. The Prophet SAW himself, and then the most righteous of the companions, and then the rest will follow. Even the order of crossing over the Sirat is something that is based upon one's Iman and Taqwa.

We learn all of these things over and over again. I hope that it has an impact on our lives. We don't want to be at the very end. We don't want to be crawling when we cross the Sirat. We don't want only our toe to be blinking on and off. Do you want that to happen to you? Obviously, you don't.

So then why don't we perfect our Salah? Why don't we wake up for Fajr and try to pray in the Masjid? Why don't we sit after the Salah and do Zikr? Why don't we perfect our Wudu, so that our Prophet SAW can recognize us?

The one who does this consistently throughout his life, In Sha Allah, Allah SWT is not going to turn away from the one who turns to him. The one who spent a lifetime doing good deeds with the intention that, 'I want our Prophet SAW to recognize me'. 'I want to crossover the Sirat in a quick manner'. Then it is impossible that Allah SWT will then turn away from that request. Because Allah SWT is Rahim, and Allah SWT is Karim. Allah STW gives when a person asks.

Then there is a phrase which is in the Musnad of Imam Ahmed, which is an authentic Hadith, and it is a very scary hadith. He said that, "The Sirat is going to be thinner than a hair, sharper than a sword, and on both sides are going to be Hooks".

The Sirat is not a massive path. Sirat is razor sharp. And it is super thin. The only way we can crossover it is by Allah SWT's mercy. The only way we can crossover it is by going at a supersonic speed, and Allah SWT will give us that strength that we need.

It is mentioned that, Salman Farsi RA said that, "The Sirat will be placed over Jahannam. It will be sharper than a sword. When the Angels will see that Sirat, they will ask Allah SWT, 'O Allah SWT, who can possibly crossover the Sirat?' Allah SWT will say, 'Whomever I choose from my creation will be able to cross that Sirat'. And then the Angels will say, 'We did not worship you O Allah SWT, the way that you deserve to be worshipped'".

This is Salman Al Farsi RA's statement. And of course, this statement cannot come from his own desire, even though he said it. The concept and the origin must go back to our Prophet SAW. The notion of even the Angels are going to be surprised.

From all of this we get the following picture that, the Sirat is a slippery path. It is something that is not easy to put your foot on. It is not firm. It is sharper than a sword. It is thinner than a hair. On either side of it, there are going to be instruments that will push or shove or catch or scratch.

We learned that people will be in utter darkness, and that the only way to get across will be the light from Allah SWT. And that they will be crossing at different speeds.

We also learn that the first person to cross will be our Prophet Muhammad SAW. And then by Allah SWT's permission, his Ummah will be the first to cross. That is what the Prophet SAW said that, "Myself and my Ummah shall be the first to crossover the Sirat". The Hadith is in Sahih Bukhari.

The Prophet SAW said that, "We are the last. And yet the first on the day of Judgement". We are the last Ummah chronologically to appear. Yet we shall be the first on the day of Judgement to have Hisab. And now we learn that we shall be first to crossover the Sirat. And we shall be first Ummah to enter Hannah. And our Prophet SAW will be the first human being to cross Sirat and enter Jannah.

This is all because of the barakah of the Prophet SAW. We thank Allah STW for being in the Ummah of our Prophet SAW. Because we get all of these perks and benefits. We would not have gotten those perks and benefits, if we were in any other Ummah.

Sirat for Disbeliever

The other issue that we need to discuss is, will the Kafir crossover the Sirat or not? The response here is that, even though some scholars said they will; The evidences seemed to be very clear that the only people that are going to get to the Sirat will be those who had the name of Islam in this world. Those who call themselves Muslims.

As for those who did not and they rejected Islam, they will not get to the Sirat in the first place. And they shall enter Jahannam through the gates of Jahannam. From the plains of the day of Judgement, the believers will go to an area where there is going to be the darkness right before the bridge.

As for those who rejected Allah STW, and they had no Iman, and they worship false gods; They shall be taken to a different area, and they shall enter Jahannam through the doors of Jahannam.

Allah SWT mentions in the Quran, "There are seven doors of Jahannam". Allah STW mentions in three verses in the Quran, Surah Nahl Verse 29, in Surah Zumar verse 72, and in Surah Ghafir verse 76, the exact same phrase, speaking to those who rejected Allah SWT, "Enter the gates of Jahannam. You shall dwell therein forever".

What this illustrates is that, anybody who enters Jahannam through the gates of Jahannam will never exit Jahannam. The believers who are sinful, and shall be punished for a period of time, they will not enter Jahannam through the gates of Jahannam.

Rather, as explained before, they will be in a different area of Jahannam. They will be in the peripheral regions that are closer to Jannah. The believers who had Iman, who lowered their heads to Allah SWT, who did some good deeds; they will never be treated like Iblees, or like Firon, or like somebody who is too arrogant to worship Allah SWT.

Even if a believer committed sins, and they deserve to be punished, their punishment will be in a separate area. They will not be dragged into Jahannam through the doors of Jahannam. Rather, they shall fall from the Sirat to a peripheral region, not to the depths of Jahannam.

As for the Munafiqun, because we don't know the details of this, and because the Munafiqun will get to the Sirat according to the text, and as the Quran says, "Munafiqun are going to be going to be in the lowest depths of Jahannam; We then make an assumption, and this is not explicit, but it is derived; that the Munafiqun will fall from the Sirat, but there fall will be different than the fall of the sinful people there.

There fall will be through different mechanisms. Maybe there's going to be separate hooks that are coming for them and they shall be dragged to the lowest of the low of hell. Even worse than those who rejected Allah SWT, are those who pretended to be Muslim, as they rejected Allah SWT.

We learn from this that the people of Iman will get to the Sirat and that majority of them, or many of them will crossover, but some of them will fall from the Sirat into the peripheral regions of Jahannam.

Expecting to Fall in to Jahannam

Now, the people who are falling into Jahannam, did they know that they're going to be falling into Jahannam? It appears, deriving it from the text, and Allah SWT knows best, that those believers who are falling into Jahannam, they are expecting to fall in.

Because the results have already been given. The examination has occurred. Hisab has taken place. The scrolls have been handed out. The Mizan has already been demonstrated. Everybody already knows their fate. And the manifestation of that fate is already known to them. At the Sirat they are going to go through it.

So, the ones who are falling into Jahannam, it's not a surprise for them. They had been told beforehand that because somebody murdered somebody, or somebody did whatever major sins, they will be going to Hell. So, they deserve to be punished.

They had been told on the plains of the Day of Judgement that you're going to go to Jahannam, because that's their punishment. So, they're expecting it. Obviously, it is understood, that as they are crossing, their heart will be earning for Jannah. But it's not going to be a surprise that they end up where they end up, because they have already been informed.

However, we can also make another assumption from the generalities of the text, that there will be people, who are told that they're going to Jahannam, and they expect to go to Jahannam, but they shall be saved by simply scratches, or by the fear of going to Jahannam. They don't actually go to Jahannam, and that their punishment was thinking that they're going to Jahannam.

Now, as the Prophet SAW said that some will be scratched but still saved. What does that indicate? It indicates there's a category of people. That their punishment was what happened on the bridge. That they thought that they are going to go to Jahannam. And they were punished in a certain manner, i.e. by the scratch from the hooks coming out, or the torcher of the thought that they're being dragged in.

In the end of the day, obviously nobody can be safe. But by Allah SWT's Qadar, it misses them, but it leaves some pain and suffering, and some scratches. That pain and suffering along with the torture of thinking that they're going to go to Jahannam, that is what their Kaffara was for the sins of this world. Eventually, they get to the end, and they shall then make it to Jannah.

Synopsis

From all of these texts, we can derive that, all three will get to the bridge. The righteous, the sinner, and the Munafiq. The Munafiq will immediately be taken out, because they are not even going to get the light. Either they fall directly or from the hook. We do not know.

In either case, whether it is a hook or whether it is falling in directly, they shall go to a different part of Jahannam, that is reserved specially for them.

Then the righteous of the believers, and the unrighteous of the believers, they will crossover the Sirat. The first batchers are going to go at the speed of light. Then speed of horses. They're going super-fast and they crossover, and they're all fine.

Slowly, people will be going less quick. Then some are going to slip, but recover. Some are going to be Injured or harmed by the hooks, but still make it; and that injury or that harm, or that terror shall be the Kaffara of the sins that they did. Even though some people will be told they are going to Jahannam, they will not, because Allah SWT's mercy is going to come in and save them at the very 11th hour.

After this, the next batch will be the unrighteous of the believers that are going to be taken from the bridge, and they're going to fall into the peripheral regions of

Jahannam. There, each one will be in accordance with his or her crimes. And each one, for the length that Allah SWT has decided for them.

Then, Shafa'a will kick in after that. Either by people, or Prophet AS, or Allah SWT. Eventually, batches by batches are going to be taken out. Those that used to pray and fast and give charity, their bodies are not going to be burnt by Jahannam. They will only feel the heat of Jahannam, and the pain and the suffering.

Now, we get to the final actual final stage of the Day of Judgement for the believers. Before entering Jannah, after crossing over the Sirat; the believers will then be left at the Qantara.

The Qantara

In the Arabic language, the Qantara is a small semicircular bridge. Generally speaking, in the medieval time, they had castles and moats. So, the bridge that covers a moat, that small little bridge that goes in U shape, that's called Qantara in Arabic. It also implies a small area at the ends of the bridge as well.

So, there will be a location called the Qantara, that's where the believers are going to be stopped at right before entering Jannah. The Qantara is therefore after the Sirat and before the actual gates of Jannah.

Who gets to the Qantara? Only the Mu'minun who are getting into Jannah. Once you've gotten to the Qantara, you are not going to be dragged back into Jahannam.

The Qantara is not mentioned in the Quran directly. It is mentioned in the Hadith. The authentic Hadith of Sahih Muslim states, the Prophet SAW said, "The believer shall be saved from the fire of hell, and they shall then be stopped or paused at a Qantara, that is between heaven and hell".

Purpose of Qantara

What is the purpose of this pausing here? The Prophet SAW said, "There is going to be Qasas between the people at the Qantara, that are going to enter Jannah about issues that happened to them in this world. Then when they have been cleansed, and they had been purified, then they should be allowed to enter Jannah".

So, the purpose of the Qantara is so settle the grudges, and the problems, and the disputes, and the unresolved issues of this world between two believers. They are both entering Jannah, but there's unresolved disputes that is going to be resolved on the Qantara.

Then the Prophet SAW made an oath, and he said, "I swear by the one who controls my life, they will know their place in Jannah more clearly than one of you knows how to get to their home".

Point being that they don't need directions. Point being that when they get to Jannah, they will intrinsically know which house is theirs and they're going to go there, and they're going to find their way.

Now, the Prophet SAW is saying, "When the believers are saved from Jahannam, they are going to be delayed upon a Qantara". This is a very explicit phrase. Those who have reached the Qantara are not going to go to Jahannam, that's it. They are now safe.

Therefore, the question arises, what is this purification for? This final batch of purification is for the trivial matters that don't deserve Jahannam. Because everybody wrongs somebody else. Who amongst us has not backbite someone else? Who amongst us has not hurt another believer? Who amongst us has not done something they shouldn't have done?

This is human nature. So, in Allah SWT's perfect justice, no one can enter Jannah until the debts have been settled. No one can enter Jannah until the smallest of misdeeds has been resolved. So, the Qantara is the final purification and the perfection of Allah SWT's justice. And it will be between people of Jannah.

This is a separate Qasas from the one of the Day of Judgement. The Qasas on the day of Judgement can decide heaven and hell, like murder or that you ruined a person's life. Or a big Zulm to the point that the perpetrator is going to Jahannam, that's already done.

We're not talking about that Qasas. That Qasas has already been done. We're talking about the trivial things that will not earn Jahannam. That will not earn Allah SWT's anger, and wrath. That type of punishment has already been decreed.

Now we get to the finer details. Now we get to the issues of he said, she said. And in Allah SWT's perfect justice that he said, she said, is not going to go unchecked. That small irritation, or nuisance, that sarcasm, that mockery, that belittling, it will not go unchecked.

Because Allah SWT says that, "I am the Malik and I am the judge. No one that has any issue with another person will go to Jannah or Jahannam until the issue is resolved". This is the Hadith in Sahih Bukhari.

Ibn Taymiyyah RA mentions that the purpose of the Qantara is very simple. That is that, only people of pure hearts will enter Jannah. So, if somebody has a grudge, they can't enter Jannah. If somebody has the pain from another, they can't enter Jannah.

If somebody has a debt that is unsettled, or somebody still feels, 'Hey that guy hurt me, and he's still here. He made it this far. To the gates of Jannah'; If somebody has that in his heart, they cannot enter Jannah.

Because Allah STW says in the Quran, in Surah Hijr Verse 47 that, "We shall remove all of the rancor in their hearts before they enter Jannah". Allah SWT shall remove all the enmity, jealousy, hatred, and rancor in their hearts. That will take place at the Qantara.

In this stage of the Qantara, the last phase before Jannah, everybody will now be able to get rid of that evil and anger. 'O Allah SWT that person he lied about me'. 'O Allah STW that person he hurt me'. Or, 'That person cracked a joke and hurt my feelings, and I was insulted'.

But overall, the person who did all of this was a righteous man. He prayed Tahajud. He gave charity. He sponsored orphans. One sarcastic comment is not going to cause him to go to Jahannam.

If somebody said one bad thing about you, you will ignore a lifetime of good they did, and you will say, 'This person hurt my feelings. He's evil. He should go to Hell'. See Allah SWT is Rahman and Rahim. And Allah SWT is the one who decides and Allah SWT is the one who is ultimately just. He can tell this person made a mistake with you, but he doesn't deserve to go to Jahannam. That's why we trust Allah SWT. We don't trust ourselves.

This is an eye opener for all of us Muslims. It shows that you're going to have problems with people, and people will have problems with you, and all of you will still enter Jannah. That's the purpose of the Qantara.

Just because you don't like somebody, means nothing about them going to heaven and hell. Stop thinking that you're playing God. Just because they did something wrong with you, that doesn't mean that their whole lives are evil.

Sometimes people become clouded by emotionality and they do something ridiculous with one person. But they were still good with all the other of mankind. So, Allah SWT will judge and decide, the wrong that this person did, is it worthy of going to Jahannam? Maybe it is. For example, somebody murdered another person and didn't repent.

If somebody murdered a human being, what if he gave $100 in charity? Murder Generally speaking deserves to go to Jahannam. That's going to be decided on the day of Judgement and that before this point in time. And that person will potentially be dragged Jahannam. And even if they were righteous, they will spend a long time in Jahannam for that murder.

But suppose a person had a fight with another person, and hearts became hard, and things were said, emotions got involved, backbiting was done etc. Who amongst us is totally free of that ever happening in our lives?

So, if overall the person was righteous, Inshallah, they will get to Jannah, but not clean. You still have the mini Hisab at the Qantara.

What will be the currency? The same thing as on the day of Judgement. That is the good deeds. Now, in this case, there is not going to be the bad deeds to go to Jahannam. Because you have now passed.

So, what will happen is that there will be adjustment in the finer details of Jannah. For example, somebody deserved a certain level of Jannah, but they did wrong to another person. So, certain perks and privileges that they had, shall now be given to the one that they wronged.

Allah SWT had given to the person a package, from that package, things will be taken out and handed over to the one that they did wrong.

Now, dear Muslims, do you want something to be taken out of the prize Allah STW has given you because of a mistake you did? Do you want some eternal blessing that Allah SWT has promised you, and He is telling you earned all of this, and you are jumping out of joy; Then you are told that, you hurt somebody's feelings. So, Allah SWT has to take this out and give it to that person.

Would you like that? Would you like an eternal blessing to be taken away and given to another, because of your own foolishness and mistake and arrogance?

That is why our Prophet SAW said that, "Make sure you resolve your problems between yourselves in this dunya, before the Akhira". That's why he said it. You don't want that to happen. Therefore, in this world, try to have as pure of heart as possible. Forgive as much as you can.

Even if somebody wrongs you, and you expect your reward from the Akhira; then you make sure you don't wrong them back. Because, you don't want to have to give up your perks and privileges to somebody else on that day.

So, Qantara demonstrates for us the infinite mercy of Allah SWT. That no injustice is ever going to go unchecked. That Allah STW is the ultimate one who will manifest justice. That's why Allah SWT said, "I am the king and I am the judge".

It also shows us that it is possible that people have wronged each other and yet still they enter Jannah. And that's exactly why Allah SWT says in Surah Hijr verse 47, "We have removed from their hearts, animosity and jealousy and hatred. And they shall be brethren".

Even in this world, they were not brethren. They were fighting. They were not talking to one another. But they were all righteous people.

Location of Qantara

The final point here is that, where exactly is the Qantara? Is it another bridge, or is it the end of the bridge of Sirat? Ibn Hajar RA references that, both opinions have been mentioned in this regard. He says that Al Qurtubi RA said that, "The Qantara is a separate mini bridge, after the bridge of Sirat". Ibn Hajar RA said, "Most likely it is the end of the Sirat, and it is not a separate bridge".

The second position is the one that most of scholars lean towards. That it does not appear to be a second bridge. Rather it appears to be a large area at end of Sirat, but before you get to the plains of Jannah.

So, before you get to the doors of Jenna, Qantara is going to be at the end of the Sirat. So, you've crossed over the Sirat and Jahannam is now behind you. And before you get to the gates of Jannah, there's going to be a massive area. That's called the Qantara. That Qantara is still connected to the Sirat.

In the end, were not certain either way. And we will all find out inshallah. We hope that Allah STW makes us of those who cross the Qantara without any issue. Once you cross the Qantara, you are now in front of the gates of Jannah.

Conclusion

This brings us to the conclusion of this book. We have finished the entire day of judgement in the relatively detailed manner. I would say this is an intermediate to advanced level that we've done, and a very thorough summary of the aspects of the Day of Judgement, from the beginning to the end, directly from the Quran and the Sunnah.

Now we get to the end of this topic, the next topic will be the description of Jannah and Jahannam. But still I want to reiterate that I hope, dear Muslims, that this knowledge that we gained from this book is not just something that you sit back and you enjoy. I hope that you think long and hard about each one of these stages. About each one of these aspects. Because it's going to happen.

We're going to see every single one of these things in front of our eyes. We shall see the Hisab, the Mizan and Sirat. We shall see the Hawd. Question now is that, do you want to be of those who are drinking from the Hawd? Do you want your Mizan to be heavy? Do you want your Scrolls to be in the right-hand side? Do you want your feet to be firm on the Sirat?

Do you want to be having light on that day? Do you want to cross Sirat at the speed of light? Do you want to crossover the Qantara?

Every one of these stages, we all know how to do them. We know how to pass the test. We know how to be amongst the highest of the high. The purpose and the reason why Allah SWT went into so much detail, and the Prophet SAW told us so many things, is that it impacts our character, our rituals, and our relationship with other people.

The religion of Islam is not just about abstract knowledge. It is meant to better our lives. To provide us purpose and meaning. To find comfort in the struggles that we're going through. To give a nobility to our lives and to make us better human beings in this world. So that we can save ourselves from all of this, and enter the pleasure of Allah SWT in the next World.

I pray that Allah SWT Allah makes us of the righteous and he blesses us to be of those who pass every one of these stages.

Assalam Waliakum wa Rahmatullahi wa Barakaatuhu,

Brothers and Sisters,

I hope you benefited from this book. If you'd like to read my other books, they are as follows;

1. Dua in Islam
2. Creation in Islam
3. Angels and Jinns in Islam
4. Adam The First Man
5. Guidance from Quran and Sunnah 1, 2 and 3
6. Seerah of Prophet Muhammad SAW 1
7. Jinns and Black Magic
8. The Signs of the Judgement Day
9. The Day of Judgement Part 1 and 2

Jazakallah Khair,

Made in the USA
Las Vegas, NV
19 March 2024

87454996R00156